WHOO INFLUENCED YOU?

WHOO INFLUENCED YOU?

THREE RELATIONSHIPS THAT TRANSFORMED MY LIFE

Curated by
Dr. George C. Fraser and Stan Matthews

Matthews and Smith Publishing
Ewing, NJ

CONTENTS

Forward

Dr. George C Fraser

What is Influence and How Do You Get It?

The world's most influential leaders, business people, and innovators know the one key characteristic to help them reach their goals and effect change. They possessed not only the ability to wield *influence*, but they were *influential*. A review of the last 20 years studying the great Black influencers in our world; Christ, Martin Luther King, Bishop Desmond Tutu, Harriet Tubman, Maya Angelo, Malcolm X, Frederick Douglas, Rosa Parks, Marcus Garvey, Earl Graves and many others - shows it wasn't just what these people did that made them influential. It wasn't because they had money, position, or authority. They were influential because of who they were or are, and the traits they possess.

Webster defines influence as the act or power of producing an effect without apparent exertion of force or direct exercise of command. Through this definition, the difference between influence and dictatorial command are delineated. Command says, "Do this because I said so and there are vile consequences if you don't." Influence says, "I am helping you to see that this is the best course of action in terms of long-term benefits for the both of us." Command can initiate change of mind, but it is externally motivated. As soon as the external consequence is lifted, the status quo is quickly resumed. Influence creates an internal shift in a person's mindset. Internal commitment is gained independent of external consequences.

The world's most influential people don't merely change other's behavior; they shift their mindsets.

Suppose you own a retail store, and an employee continues to not greet customers in line with your culture. Command says,

"Do this or you'll get fired or written up." Influence says, "Let me show you why this is important to your success and mine." The employee who is commanded to greet customers will do so while he or she thinks you are watching. Your customers will see through the veneer, as well. The employee who is influenced will begin to sincerely greet customers regardless of your presence because an internal shift has occurred.

WHAT THE WORLD NEEDS IS FEWER COMMANDERS AND MORE INFLUENCERS!

YOU can be an influencer. In fact, you already are. AND you can grow your ability to become even more influential once you identify and understand your potential to be influential in relation to:
- Achieving business success.
- Expanding your leadership impact.
- Realizing a needed outcome for a worthy cause.
- Building others as you help them make a significant mark on the world.
- Gaining admission into a prestigious MBA or graduate program.
- Attaining your dream in your personal life.

Change is temporary. Shift is permanent. Grow Your Influence. Expand Your Influence

TRUE INFLUENCE IS BASED IN AN EMOTIONAL CONNECTION

A crucial aspect of influence is the emotional connection you make with people. True influence involves building trust and a relationship, getting those people to align their views and values with your own for long-term gain. Short-term change doesn't rely as much upon emotional connection, instead it uses other tactics like reasoning, manipulation, or coercion.

You only have to look at your own experiences to see the difference. If someone threatens or coerces you to get you to do something, you might do it at the moment, but long-term resentment means you'll revert to the previous behavior as soon as you can.

On the other hand, if a friend asks you to change your behavior in some way, you're much more likely to do so – more importantly, you're much more likely to *want* to do so. You're emotionally invested in that person and want to see him or her succeed to the point that you'll help them however and wherever you can.

With a rich background in psychology and human behavior, researcher Dr. Karen Keller states that: TRUE INFLUENCE happens at a deeper internal level." This sets you apart. She goes on to say: *"Unless an internal shift occurs change will not last."*

BECOME A WORLD CHANGER, GROW AS AN INFLUENCER

- Harriet Tubman shifted our mindset about Black courage and commitment
- Marcus Garvey–shifted the Black world's mindset about Black self- help
- Martin Luther King —shifted the world's mindset about leadership.
- Archbishop Desmond Tutu-shifted the world's mindset about what it means to truly forgive.
- Earl Graves -shifted our mindset about Black businesses
- Your Mom/Dad—hopefully shifted your mindset on how to treat others with love and kindness.

Whether you are called to shift the world's mindset on the global stage, or through leading your small business, mentoring or by parenting your children, your legacy will be seen in those you influenced deeply. Growing your influence isn't just important for personal success. Your future depends on it.

Whoo Influenced You? is 20 exciting and informative stories of everyday people just like you whose lives were impacted by influencers. Why? Because they were open and listened!

DR. GEORGE C. FRASER

A SLICE OF MY LIFE AND THE 4 INFLUENCERS THAT CHANGED IT

"It's not who you know, but who knows you and what is it they know about you"

If you want to meet influential people, you must be where influential people are, then find a way to serve and add value to their life first.

I've always had a dream list of influential people I wanted to meet, one of them was Earl G. Graves, the iconic founder of Black Enterprise Magazine (BE). He was an early role model of mine, having been born and raised in Bed Stuy, Brooklyn, NY, a decade before me. I let my dream be known to a few of my well-connected and influential Cleveland friends. In 1985, my influential friend Carole Hoover (President of the Cleveland Growth Association) recommended me to become the volunteer Cleveland Co-Chairman of a 7-city networking tour Earl G. Graves was planning. It was a year away, a lot of hard work but I eagerly took the assignment unconditionally. What I didn't know at the time, the seeds for a new dream were planted. In September of 1986, the BE Networking Forum in Cleveland launched with great success. Nearly five hundred Black professionals attended this corporate sponsored, "paid" event to hear Mr. Graves speak on the state of Blacks in the business world and why building networking skills was critically important. Business cards flew across the room in a networking frenzy. It was the first event of its kind in Cleveland, and it sparked something in me, and changed my life. I was proud of the event; Mr. Graves was ecstatic. What was to come 8 years later was a complete surprise. More on that later.

The BE Networking Forum reminded me of an exciting time in my life like my famous New Year's Eve parties and my days as an entrepreneur selling Black encyclopedias' doing well while doing good. Earl Graves had always been a visionary and a leader in bringing Black professionals together to network, do business, and empower one another economically. On reflection, I found that I had long shared his sense of wanting to strengthen our community. And ever since my days as the founder of a neighborhood male baby-sitting, house cleaning and lawn care service I had instinctively grasped the power of networking.

The success of the BE Networking Forum brought many disparate and dormant thoughts to the forefront of my consciousness. I sensed that there must be millions of Black professionals in search of entrepreneurial and networking skills. The paper cuts on my hands from flying business cards were also graphic evidence of the enthusiasm. And so, in the months and years that followed, I began designing my own plan.

At first, it was a subconscious process, fleeting thoughts finding one another and clumping together. But when it became more and more apparent that my future as a Ford Motor automobile dealer was not a promising one because of the depressed auto market, I consciously began developing the concept that would be both my greatest career gamble and my most exhilarating challenge.

In mid-1988, I graduated from the Ford Dealership Development Program, one of 12 African Americans nationwide selected in mid1986 of which I got through another inside connection at Ford headquarters. I made a lot of new friends, but this influential corporate titan had a profound impact on my life, **Don Peterson**, President of Ford Motor Company, more about him later. I declined to pursue a dealership of my own and Ford was not happy. For the first time in twenty years, I had no corporate job, no income, no company car, and no benefits. I did have a large mortgage, a very puzzled wife, two growing sons, ideas, dreams, and visions. But none-the-less I had to get started.

Earlier I had begun testing my plan by staging the first of a series of monthly networking forums for Black professionals in Cleveland with my new business partner **Greg Williams** an influential Cleveland nightclub owner and promoter. The

Black Enterprise network forum had been primarily a social affair. Mine was strictly business—a "Party with a Purpose"—at least in theory. My idea was to bring in top Black speakers of national stature to address a wide variety of topics that would champion personal and professional development to include building wealth, businesses, and networking skills throughout the Black community. I felt there was a need to encourage interdependence and a greater sense of trust and shared goals among Black professionals. I wanted to bring them together on a regular basis to discuss these common themes, and to develop a unified agenda for the success of all Black people, but I needed a corporate sponsor.

I staged my first SuccessNet (Success Through Networking) Forum on January 18, 1988. My close friend Les Brown was just starting his speaking career, so he was the first featured speaker, and the Ford Motor Company, with which I had maintained a good relationship with President Don Peterson, signed on for a two-year sponsorship with an investment of $100,000. The first forum was profitable, it had a turnout of more than 500 people and convinced me that I was on to something.

Even as I completed my final year of training with Ford, I staged monthly SuccessNet forums in Cleveland, they became a networker's paradise, not to mention a pretty good place to learn and meet influencers. Celebrity speakers included Danny Glover, Geoffrey Holder, Susan Taylor, Earl Graves, Louis Ruckeyser, Carole Simpson, Ron Brown, Tony Brown, John H. Johnson, Denis Waitley, Dennis Kimbro, Wally "Famous" Amos, James Earl Jones, Stedman Graham and of course, Don Peterson, President of Ford just to name a few. The forums attracted a wide array of corporate sponsors eager to be the official radio station, airline, newspaper, or hotel for all the events, which drew up to fifteen hundred professionals for cocktails, hors d'oeuvres, networking, inspiration, training, and enlightenment.

Each meeting began with a recitation of a group mantra that went: *"Success lives in Cleveland because Success lives where I live. We must be willing to share our Success and to help others*

Succeed. Each one must reach one and teach one." I still use this mantra to this day when I close many of speeches.

SuccessNet began as a sideline while I was still in the Ford training program. When I graduated from the program and left Ford's corporate fold, I immediately launched my own full-time business—from the extra bedroom in our house. The assets of SuccessSource, were not ones that most bankers would embrace as strong collateral. I had my "Soul-O-Dex" Rolodex; my close friend Gregory Williams, who left his business to join me in my dream; and the monthly bills to inspire me.

In truth, the "Soul-O-Dex" was strong collateral, because it contained the names of some very influential people whom I had met over the years and with whom I had developed trusting relationships. To finance my new business, I made a private stock offering. And I made it to key people, many of whom were among the power elite of Cleveland. Eighteen of them were CEOs of major companies. These same people helped me get advertising for the second product to come out of SuccessSource, the coffee table quality *Success Guides; the Networking Guide to Black Resources in Greater Cleveland...*which years later expanded to 7 urban centers where I had a network of great friends and contacts. We were well on our way.

I don't want to give the impression that this was a cakewalk because it was not. Although I had many wonderful supporters, financially and spiritually, my new business suffered all the travails encountered by most small minority enterprises—principally, the inability to get capital for growth. My partner and I worked virtually without salary for several years. More than once, I had to go to friends for either cash or counsel. But that is why networking is so important. It provides a foundation of support.

It was during this period that I received some very bad and very good news from back home in Brooklyn. My youngest brother Joseph was killed in a drug deal gone bad, and my sister Emma was completing her course work for a master's from Harvard. It was both a stunning blow and a joyous victory. We had grown up together in the same orphanages, and foster homes. Emma and I had shared values, experiences, and choices, yet Joseph's choices led to a life of crime and drugs, Emma and my choices led to the highest form of educational and business achievement. It was lack of good choices and results in my own family that provided me the determination to continue down my new business path and make SuccessSource work as I had originally envisioned it.

I come from essentially the same background as millions of other Blacks of my generation. And I have learned something that I believe is of benefit to all people. I have learned that our choice of the people and relationships in our life will help determine our life. "Your network will determine your net worth". I've learned Blacks have a 5000-year legacy of success that runs contrary to the media images of slavery, welfare, crime, drugs. And we have the potential to much more than sing, dance, play football, baseball, or basketball.

***

IN JUST ONE MOMENT, ONE PERSON OR INTERACTION CAN CHANGE YOUR LIFE

In retrospect, I view my interaction with Earl Graves, and the BE Networking Forum in 1986 as Part 1 of a turning point in my life. Part 2 came in July 1994 when Earl Graves enthusiastically endorsed my "magnum-opus" book *Success Runs in Our Race: The Complete Guide to Effective Networking in the Black Community,* he made it BE's first book excerpt and put me on the cover. At that point my business and career took off…and the rest is history. Mr. Graves and I had a very productive long relationship, he died in April 2020, just as the Covid pandemic started. His son Earl "Butch" Graves Jr. has done an incredible job at taking BE to the 21st Century.

What I find striking about that period is the fact that although my family's entire financial future and quality of life was at risk due to my business venture, I was not stressed out about it. All my high-paying, high-visibility corporate jobs had been high-anxiety. Even though I was working within the security of the corporate fold, I had always been stressed about preserving that security. And I was always under pressure to fit into a corporate culture that for all its efforts at diversity and inclusion it still was still struggling to make the mix work.

I continue to be a wing-walker by comparison, traipsing on the edge of a deadly fall without a parachute. But I have confidence because I know that my strength does not come from a corporation's ample assets, from a big office or a comfortable pension. It comes from within and my very ample network of wonderful and protective relationships. And I know the same can be true of you and nearly every one of any culture, regardless of circumstances, for it is not how you start, it's how you finish. We are a people with passion and creativity in abundance. The challenge is to channel those assets into a form of social entrepreneurialism that can produce goods and services to fulfill the needs of our communities. Technology has dramatically improved within the last two decades, but the challenges remain the same: doing what you love with people that you love. That is why my old company, SuccessSource, has morphed into SuccessNet, then into FraserNet, and now a virtual nation named FraserNation, a network of 1.3 million people, influencers, friendships, relationships, and allies, to include human and intellectual assets around the globe engaged in strategic alliances, joint ventures, and partnerships. We have gathered annually for over 20 years at the *PowerNetworking Conference* to renew our friendships.

Bottom Line: Aside from my family, especially my sister Dr. Emma Fraser-Pendleton, my wife Nora Jean and children, and a host of great friends, four key people influenced my career path and thus my purpose: Carole Hoover, Earl Graves, Greg Williams, and Don Petersen. Earl and Greg have passed on to take their throne next to our God. Carole and Don (95 years old) remain good friends.

Dr. George C. Fraser *is Chairman and CEO of FraserNet, Inc., a company he founded 32 years ago to lead a global networking and economic development movement for people of African descent. Born in Brooklyn, NY, he spent 20 years in Executive leadership positions with Procter & Gamble, United Way and Ford Motor Company before starting his own business, FraserNet Inc. in 1987. He is the author of 6 best-selling books including: Success Runs in Our Race, and most recently, Mission Unstoppable: Extraordinary Stories of Failure's Blessings, a book he co-authored with Les Brown.*

STAN MATTHEWS

THE SAINTS WHO SHAPED THE MAN

Maylene Andrews gave me life and transformed my life at a very early and important stage. My beloved mother will always be my primary source of inspiration, motivation and prosperity. Mom prepared my spirit and mind for success with a constant demand of excellence and a cascade of compliments and encouragement. Mom provided the unconditional love and guidance that created an indomitable spirit and unwavering confidence that I could be do and have all things in god's name and by his power.

Mom was a bundle of energy, joy and strength. She was adored respected and feared by family, friends and colleagues. Her 5 brothers each recounted altercations they were in as children and seeing their younger sister come flying into the fray to defend her older brothers with fire and fearlessness. Mom was a respected and honored person in here community and in her family. She was the loving mother of my sister Coco and I and the 6th of 8 children. She was both feared and loved for her sharp tongue and quick wit and strong mind. My mom loved, protected, and shaped my mind for excellence and success continuously.

Mom's most important gift was to share her unbreakable faith. Mom and I loved to share our favorite scriptures. We would go on for hours speaking about the God's grace and mercy. She taught me never to worry about my goals because she firmly believed that, "God's will is God's bill. She shared her mom's story that we were stolen from Africa and brought to Guyana South America and that we were members of the Great Ashanti Nation. I can feel the pride and power rising in my mind and spirit even as I share this writing with you now.

Mom taught me mental mastery and a determination that still shapes my approach and practice as an entrepreneur. She taught that excellence was the only standard and that doing well in business was good but doing good and doing well was even better. She taught me to always provide greater value than the client and customer paid for with love and good humor. Her baked seafood gumbo was legendary and I feel myself getting hungry for some right now.

Mom and my Grandma Beatrice taught me to that my network was my net worth long before I made that my primary marketing message. She kept a small book with the names and addresses of each of her nursing clients and would send birthday greetings and prosperity prayers to each of them. She reminded me over and over again that if I got the people problem right I would never have a money problem in business and boy was she right.

Maylene Andrews transformed my mind and gave me a confidence that borders on positive arrogance. Mom asked me to memorize Psalm 23 Chapter because it stated in plain language that God guides and provides with love. This lesson has reinforced my positive view of who I was and whose I was for the rest of my life. No one could ever again devalue or undervalue my self-love and self-worth.

My mom transformed my love for family as a foundation principal in a well lived life. She would prepare Sunday Dinner with the expertise of a chef and a love that created an amazingly great tasting meal. Mom, my sister Collette {aka Coco} prayed for each other before and after each meal and Sunday afternoons were a treasure trove of laughter, positive storytelling and life lessons that my sister and I never forgot. The three of us will have and unbreakable love. To this day tears well up when Sade's, "Nothing can come between us plays".

My mom transformed my life with the example of her love for my Grandpa Benjamin Andrews. My grandfather was a stern and somewhat intimidating figure. He was slow to speak and quick to punish wrongdoing and steadfast in his defense and love for his children and grandchildren. My mom loved her dad dearly and did everything with the singular goal of pleasing her daddy.

Mom's most important gift was her love and gratitude. She taught me to love like God loves and to give and forgive like

God gives and forgives. Mom taught me to be grateful before I received the thing or experience I was praying for. She said celebrate the vision long before the reality. She said God was the loving force that in everything, everyone and everywhere. He is with me and with you always.

My mom transformed my life for the positive with her example of a life well lived, a steadfast faith that protected and guided her and a love for god and family that was unbreakable. She occupies a sacred place in my spirit, heart and mind. I give her thanks for standing in the gap and providing "true north" directions for success in life. All that I am and ever wished to be was co-signed and celebrated and encouraged by my greatest fan, my mom. Thank you, Mommy.

Lillian Matthews profoundly transformed my life at a very early and important stage. My beloved paternal grandmother was the personification of love for me from my 3rd birthday to my 7th birthday when I was ultimately reunited with my beloved mother Maylene Andrews. Grandma Lillian provided a special unconditional love and that taught me that love is the greatest force for change and for good in this world.

Grandma Lillian was a beloved, respected and honored person in her community and in her family. She was the mother of 7 children and a wife for more than 50 years. She was loved for her warm loving spirit and an unlimited kindness that impacted and warmed the hearts of anyone she came in contact with. My Grandma Lillian loved protected me and shaped my humanity and concern for others in a permanent and awesome way.

One of Grandma's first and most important gifts was to share the wisdom of learning to practice self-care and self-love. She also showed me how to enjoy special treats and the sacred science of "me time". Among our "me time" special treats was the heavenly nectar of coffee and a slice of lemon meringue pie. I can taste it right now.

Grandma Lillian taught me how to lovingly and respectfully relate with people. Her instructions and example still shapes my approach to relationships as an entrepreneur. She told me that doing well in business was good but doing good and doing well was even better. She taught me to always provide greater value than the client and customer paid for with love and good humor.

My Grandma taught me to that my network was my net worth long before I made that my primary marketing message. She kept a small book with the names and addresses of each of her relatives and close friends and would send birthday greetings and prosperity prayers to each of them. She reminded me over and over again that if I got the people problem right I would never have a money problem in business and boy was she right.

Lillian Matthews transformed my heart and mind, gave me strength to exercise love and concern for others that guides my conduct to this day. Grandma asked me to memorize Genesis Chapter 1 verses 26-28 because it stated in plain language that God created man and woman in his image and likeness and gave them authority to rule. This lesson has reinforced my positive view of who I was and whose I was for the rest of my life. No one could ever again devalue or undervalue my self-love and self-worth.

My beloved paternal grandmother transformed my love for family as a foundation principal in a well lived life. She would prepare Sunday Dinner for more than 12 people on a routine basis and everyone was overfed and happy. We prayed for each other before and after each meal and Sunday afternoons were a treasure trove of laughter, positive storytelling and life lessons that my aunts, uncles and cousins prioritized in their weekly calendar and rarely ever missed.

My Grandma Lillian transformed my life with the example of her love for my Grandpa Cecil Matthews the 1st. My grandfather was a confident highly adventurous man. He was always thinking, always exploring and always ready to share the next idea and great adventure. My Grandma Lillian was the "only" person with enough love force to take his attention away from his life as a guide in the dangerous rain forest and river valleys of Guyana's interior region. They were inseparable and an amazing team.

My Grandma Lillian most important gift was her faith. She taught me to be grateful before I received the thing or experience I was praying for. She said celebrate the vision long before the reality. She said God was the loving force at that resided in everything, everyone and everywhere. She told me that he was ever present, ever powerful and that I should fear no one or nothing because god would always be with me. I have never forgotten and I never will. He is with me and with you always.

My Grandma transformed my life for the positive with her example of a love well lived, a steadfast faith that protected and guided her and a love for god and family that was unbreakable. She occupies a special and sacred place in my spirit, heart and mind. I give her thanks for providing a priceless love supreme experience. Thank you Grandma Lillian. Thank you so much!

Beatrice Andrews transformed my life at a very early and important stage. My beloved maternal grandmother prepared my spirit and mind for success from my 3rd birthday to my 7th birthday when I was ultimately reunited with my beloved mother Maylene Andrews. Grandma Beatrice provided the unconditional love and guidance that created an indomitable spirit unwavering confidence that I could be do and have all things in god's name and by his power.

Grandma was a respected and honored person in here community and in her family. She was the mother of 7 children and a wife for more than 50 years. She was both feared and loved for her mastery of herbal science which she had no formal training but exercised absolute mastery she learned from her mother who was an even more legendary figure in my community. My Grandma loved protected and shaped my mind for excellence and success continuously.

One of Grandma's first and most important gifts was to share that I was a member of the Ashanti Nation. She said we were stolen from Africa and brought to Guyana South America. She gave me a gold ring with my initials carved in the template and asked me to promise never to betray the people of gold, The Great Ashanti Nation. I can feel the pride and power rising in my mind and spirit even as I share this writing with you now.

Grandma Beatrice taught me market place mastery that still shapes my approach and practice as an entrepreneur. She told me that doing well in business was good but doing good and doing well was event better. She taught me to always provide greater value than the client and customer paid for with love and good humor. Her baked bread was legendary and people came from miles around our village on Sunday afternoons to buy her equally legendary fried fish and pine tarts.

My Grandma taught me to that my network was my net worth long before I made that my primary marketing message. She kept a small book with the names and addresses of each of her clients and would send birthday greetings and prosperity prayers to each of them. She reminded me over and over again that if I got the people problem right I would never have a money problem in business and boy was she right.

Beatrice Andrews transformed my mind and gave me a confidence that borders on positive arrogance. Grandma asked me to memorize Genesis Chapter 1 verses 26-28 because it stated in plain language that God created man and woman in his image and likeness and gave them authority to rule. This lesson has reinforced my positive view of who I was and whose I was for the rest of my life. No one could ever again devalue or undervalue my self-love and self-worth.

My beloved maternal grandmother transformed my love for family as a foundation principal in a well lived life. She would prepare Sunday Dinner for more than 25 people on a routine basis and everyone was overfed and happy. We prayed for each other before and after each meal and Sunday afternoons were a treasure trove of laughter, positive storytelling and life lessons that my aunts, uncles and cousins prioritized in their weekly calendar and rarely ever missed.

My Grandma transformed my life with the example of her love for my Grandpa Benjamin Andrews. My grandfather was a stern and somewhat intimidating figure. He was slow to speak and quick to punish wrongdoing and steadfast in his defense and love for his children and grandchildren. My Grandma was the "only" person who could soften everything about my grandfather instantly and almost magically. They were inseparable and an amazing team.

My Grandma's most important gift was her faith. She taught

me to be grateful before I received the thing or experience I was praying for. She said celebrate the vision long before the reality. She said God was the loving force that in everything, everyone and everywhere. She said rain was Gods loving tears that helped to bring harvest and abundance. She told me that he was ever present, ever powerful and that I should fear no one or nothing because god would always be with me. I have never forgotten and I never will. He is with me and with you always.

My Grandma transformed my life for the positive with her example of a life well lived, a steadfast faith that protected and guided her and a love for god and family that was unbreakable. She occupies a special and sacred place in my spirit, heart and mind. I give her thanks for standing in the gap and providing "true north" directions for success in life. Thank you Grandma.

***

This love letter of dedication is a thank you which looks back, which observes the present and honors the future at the same time. My prayer is a prayer of blessing for each of those persons who poured into my life and positively impacted and influenced me to succeed. This is not a comprehensive list but I am hopeful it is comprehensive enough to recognize the people who shaped my life for the better.

Heartfelt thanks to my Super Mom Maylene Andrews, Leon Matthews my biological dad, Leroy Andrews my maternal uncle and spiritual dad thank you. Heartfelt thanks, to my maternal grandmother, Beatrice Andrews, paternal grandmother Lillian Matthews to my maternal grandfather Benjamin Andrews and my paternal grandfather Cecil Matthews. Heartfelt thanks to my beloved sisters Collette "Coco" Matthews and Ms. Ingrid West, to my brothers Anthony J.Moss, Hosia Reynolds, Coley Freeman, Darryl Love, Ralph Henderson, Martin Davis and many others too numerous to mention. True friends are the gifts that keep giving. Thanks you for lending an ear, a thoughtful word, a kindness, a laugh, an unbreakable bond and a covenant.

Heartfelt thanks to my many mentors some of whom I have claimed without asking or meeting including Dr. John

Henrik Clarke, Dr. Martin Luther King Jr. Malcolm X, Frederick Douglass, Dr. Leonard Jeffries, Frederick Douglass, President Abraham Lincoln, President Nelson Mandela, President Barack Obama, PM Abiy Ahmed, Dr. George C. Fraser, Mr. Jim Rohn, Reverend Ike, Mr. Hilton Davis Esq. and Mr. Cedric Barrow.

Heartfelt thanks to my aunts and uncles and to my super cousins Mr. Dennis Andrews, Michael West, Mr. Wendell West, and Mr. Orrin King. Heartfelt thanks to my circle of friends. My friends are as countless as the sands on a vast beach and as significant to me as my very heartbeat. Heartfelt thanks to Michelle and Jenneh the amazing women who provided love and companionship and four children who are the treasure of my life.

Heartfelt thanks to Candace, Andre, Zsari and Elijah. My children you are my treasure and my greatest joy. I leave you a prayer of prosperity and legacy of success and hope. I celebrate my grandchildren and their grandchildren though unborn, but shaped by praying, my speaking and my loving each of the four of you in an everlasting unconditional way.

Infinite blessings of prosperity. Love Dad.

Stan Matthews is the proud dad of four wonderful children 3 of whom are college grads and professionals. Family is everything to me. Nothing is more important. I am the founder and the CEO of Matthews Business Network. MBN is a national platform with global reach. MBN has 2216 Black and Brown CEOs committed to taking advantage of the 1.6 trillion in black purchasing power our community has at its disposal annually. MBN also provides Black and Brown Entrepreneurs, Professionals, Creative Artists and Authors the opportunity to share the unique value of their products and services in our national professional network and on CNN, MSNBC, ESPN and MTV and the other premier networks on the Comcast platform.

SHIRLEY MUHAMMAD

I NEVER WOULD HAVE MADE IT

A Sharecropper's Daughter

My dad, James Tolbert was a sharecropper from Troy, Alabama, born on January 29, 1929. He was the second of four children, born to Jesse and Gussie Tolbert. He was the only male child in the family of three sisters. My dad's mother is Cherokee Indian, and my grandfather's heritage is from Africa and descendants of slaves. My father and the entire family worked on a sharecropping farm in Troy, Alabama.

In the rural south, sharecropping enabled white landowners to re-establish a labor force, which gave Black people no financial security. By the early 20th century, cotton had become king, and the labor of picking cotton in the Deep South was intense and focus driven. Since cotton had become a main commodity, sharecroppers spent many hours picking cotton. It was common for workers to labor in cotton fields anywhere from 12-14 hours a day.

My dad and his family faced many adversities in the heat with little to no compensation. My aunt shared disturbing stories where fainting, strokes and exhaustion were a common occurrence on cotton plantations. She told me how she fainted on several times while working in those hot and humid cotton fields.

During his teen years picking cotton, my dad, like my aunt witnessed the harshness of sharecropping. He knew he had to leave home to obtain a better life but was not sure how to leave a place he always called home. His self-determination spoke to his desire wanting to leave the south. Deep within, he knew the injustice of sharecropping were plain inhuman. There was a human need to escape Jim Crow laws that gave birth to sharecropping.

Dad finally decided to leave the south and enlist in the U.S.

army at an early age to escape Jim Crow and all its devices. Enlisting into the military and taking care of the family, served as one of the greatest freedom tickets for my dad to experience social and economic liberation.

After enlisting in the army my dad sent money back home to the family in Troy to ensure that upon his return to Alabama they would leave the south, head east and never return to the land of evil inopportunity. During his military tenure, he fought in the Korean War, which lasted for three long years, causing the lives of thousands of American and Asians soldiers. His right leg got crushed from the overturn in a military jeep army truck causing him to lose a leg. After the accident, he was flown back to Walter Reed Hospital to receive a prosthetic leg. The jeep accident resulted in an honorable discharge for my father, however, the loss of his leg impacted his life. On March 4, 1956, my mom and dad were married in Pittsburgh, Pennsylvania and my oldest sister was born on June 22nd of that same year.

My father's sharecropping experience influenced my understanding of the importance of not holding on to a sharecroppers' mentality. Unlike my dad who did not receive a formal education, my educational journey began with studies in sociological research and journalism, and later I received a master's degree in accountancy to become a tax accountant. My education created a foundation for me, yet I yearned for more of something that was missing; something that would make my education work for me, which I later discovered was understanding the science of business. Though my father never received his forty acres with a mule; deep in my heart, I still desired my own *"forty acres with a mule.*

His invaluable experience taught me not to settle for a regular (J.O.B. "Just over Broke"). Rather, his life experience encouraged me to pull myself up from deep within, to become an entrepreneur that my father would be pleased with. His experience allowed me to envision becoming the best version of my business self, as opposed to working eight hours for someone else. The 9-5 rat race we call a "job" sadly reminds me of how we sell ourselves short, robbing us of our own freedom to do for ourselves. In a way, we are still sharecropping, but today with some form of compensation for creature comforts, only.

Back in the day, sharecropping was just another form of slavery, an economic tool that kept my father, along with millions of Black families in the South dependent on white landowners. Only after leaving the south was my father able to experience upward mobility and to create a life for himself without having to look over his shoulder in fear of being run down and kidnapped by Klansmen.

Today, I have been a business owner for twenty-three years. I recognize I am a work in progress and overtime, I have shed my sharecropper's mentality, by removing the mental shackles of dependence and replacing it with a wonderful "do-for-self" business acumen.

THE LIFE AND LEGACY OF A HIP HOP MOGUL

My son, born Dwayne Lamar Tolbert on November 13, 1971, had been a successful businessperson as far back as I can remember. Selling a variety of shoelaces and tennis shoes, his entrepreneurial journey began in middle school. After high school, Dwayne chose not to attend college, something that I genuinely wanted for him. One day in our conversation about college, he said to me, "What can they teach me?" He proved to me that he had big dreams and he was determined to make his dreams come true.

Dwayne decided to attend school to become a successful travel agent and at 19, he owned a fragrance business. During the beginning stages of the Hip Hop era, he was attracted to the music industry, and soon became a worldwide Hip Hop promoter, networking with music moguls, Russell Simmons, Ron Isley and Charlie Wilson and many others.

He later created 360 Entertainment, a promotion business, which I was impressed with his business skills. In the gospel industry, he collaborated with legendary great Shirley Ceasar. Another thing that was an inspiration for me was his ability to give back to the community. Under the 360 Entertainment umbrella, he created the dynamic Hip Hop Music awards to give back to the community. It was his desire for Black youth to have their own BET awards in their own neighborhoods. It also served as an alternative to combat the selling of drugs in the Black community.

I was mesmerized by my son's ability to grow his 360 Entertainment so quickly. This made me take a second look at his business strategies. While I was working a nine to five "job," my son already had an office in the business district area of down Pittsburgh located on Smithfield Street. I was convinced then there was something incredibly special about my son's business talents. By then, he had already accepted the teaching of the Most Honorable Elijah Muhammad, which had a significant impact on his life.

I noticed that besides practicing a discipline lifestyle, the teachings also taught my son about the Muhammad Economic Blueprint, an economic program designed to help Black people to help themselves in the battle to create jobs, as well as end poverty and want. As a mother, to witness my son's life-changing transformation influenced me. He led a disciplined life and became a businessperson simultaneously. I was totally enamored with the Nation of Islam's impact on Dwayne's life. The teachings of the Most Honorable Elijah Muhammad had become a redeeming quality for his life.

On December 4, 2011, my son transitioned from this earthly life, due to a blood clot that traveled to his heart, at the age of forty, the age of spiritual maturity. His transition acknowledged that his work was complete on this plane of existence. His legacy, and business talents will forever live in my heart. He is still my rock, my inspiration, and motivation. May the peace and blessings of Allah be upon Him.

The Martyr

My grandson, Dwayne McGhee Tolbert-Muhammad, (February 3, 1989 – May 4, 2018), a splitting image of Nipsey Hustle.

There lies the makeshift memorial spot created by Dwayne's hommies at the exact location where he was gunned down in front of the Nation of Islam Muhammad Study Group in Pittsburgh, Pennsylvania. This is the location where he worshiped and propagated the teachings of the Most Honorable Elijah Muhammad under the leadership of the Honorable Louis Farrakhan and his faith as a Muslim.

It is safe to say that May 4, 2018, impacted lives and changed them forever. The sudden death of Dwayne resonated from the streets of Pittsburgh, Philadelphia to Chicago and spread throughout the entire world like a wildfire. Hundreds of thousands knew Dwayne as the other side of 360 Entertainment is the "real estate" of the legendary worldwide Hip Hop Awards, founded by his father. Dwayne Muhammad (PBUH) also mention as one of the three people who influenced me. Dwayne Muhammad, Jr was an expert salesperson, a characteristic and personality he inherits from his father. He shadowed his father for many years to learn the hip hop industry. He was very philanthropic wanting to see an end to poverty everywhere. There were so many levels to him and so much land that he had covered in his short 29 years of life.

My grandson, checked in on his sibling as requested by his father, who seemed to know that he had a destiny on the "Wheel."

My grandson will always remain a martyr because he was assassinated with the Final Call Newspaper in his hand. Dwayne was a representation of peace, which sounds like an oxymoron especially in inner city of Pittsburgh neighborhoods. What young Black man do you know who dare conduct business in a community with and have camaraderie with a known rival person?

Dwayne, although not perfect by any means, he made sure he was connected to his family especially all his siblings. He was very instrumental in teaching his little sister to cover up as a female Muslim. Every now and then I would get that special call from Dwayne just to see how I was doing.

There is a saying that leaders are born not taught, and to whom much is given, much is required. Dwayne wore many hats, always with the intent for the greater good of his family the Nation of Islam and community. Such an activist must be celebrated by their actions, simply leading by example, which was evident at his vigils. Not only was the Janazah (Funeral) Service completely packed at the Community Empowerment Association, located in the Homewood section of Pittsburgh, Pennsylvania but the Nation of Islam Student Minister Victor Muhammad spoke, and the Regional Delaware Valley Student Laborers attended out of Muhammad Mosque #12, located in Philadelphia, Pennsylvania, the broader Islamic communities were present, community activists, his peers and family and friends and colleagues. Security was very tight inside and out-side and everyone in attendance was searched. The Nation of Islam provided the security deemed for a Fallen Solider.

My grandson, started a movement that must be continued, but not just in Pittsburgh, worldwide. The world can benefit from more activists, more entrepreneurs, and people willing to give back and build in their communities. Dwayne's legacy will live through his children, children's, children's children. Through Voices of Black Mothers United, a national organization and movement founded by Dr, Robert Woodson, and founder of the Woodson Center. VBMU is a group of Black mothers who have lost loved ones to Black-on-Black homicides within their own communities. We advocate, intervene with families and communities, and promote positive policing.

My grandson transitioned making a change in his life and accepted Islam. His change touched many people.

*"...For me, understanding the platform I have and who it speaks to, it's about being strategic. We can't stand on the corner with the bull horn and preach, that isn't going to work. We have to be strategic and make an impact through influence. I wanted to redefine the lifestyle and what we view as important."- **Nipsey Hussle***

> *"Life is Like Accounting. 'Our Happiness Credits and Sorrows Always Debits"*

Vaibhav Singh

Gratefulness to Master Fard Muhammad, for informing me that I will never have to want for anything in righteousness. Gratefulness to the Most Honorable Elijah Muhammad for the Muhammad Economic Blueprint. Gratefulness to the Honorable Minister Louis Farrakhan for singing my Swan Song so that I can live.

In loving memory of my son, Dwayne Tolbert Muhammad. My best friend, my business partner and who has my motherly love, unconditionally and who was always there for me, regardless. In loving memory of my grandson, Dwayne Tolbert McGhee-Muhammad Jr, the martyr. In loving memory of my mother, Thalia K. Tolbert, who taught me to get an education because no one can take it away. In loving memory of my father, James L. Tolbert, thank you for letting me see you read *Think and Grow Rich by Napoleon Hill*. In loving memory of my oldest sister Gussie L. Tolbert who encouraged me when I did not have the courage. In loving memory of my beautiful cousins. In loving memory of my aunts and uncles for teaching me life's lessons. In loving memory of my maternal and paternal grandmother and my maternal and paternal grandfather, whose shoulders I stand on.

Gratefulness to my Aunt Mary Booth, who is blessed to celebrate her 90th birthday on May 30, 2021. To my brother who is one of the stubbornness persons that I know, to my sister who is the version of my mother.

Gratefulness to my friends, colleagues and the Mighty MGT & GCC, too many to mention and the FOI that have been my brothers and protectors. Gratefulness to my mentors. Some of them I have claimed without asking or meeting, including Harriet Tubman (PBUH), Mother Clara Muhammad (PBUH), Mother Kadijah Farrakhan Muhammad and Mother Tynetta Muhammad (PBUH) and Sister Dr. Ava Muhammad.

To the Mathew Business Network and its many members, far too many to name. Dr. George C Frasier who my son introduced me to and explained to me that networking is the keys to business success. Dr. Robert Woodson of the Woodson Center. A Black Philanthropist that supports the "least of these" in most neighborhoods across the United States. Voices of Black Mothers United, a national movement that advocate, intervene with families and communities, and promote positive policing regarding families that lost loved ones because of Black-on-Black homicides in their own communities.

Gratefulness to my grandchildren, Darelle Tolbert McGhee -Muhammad, the twin brother of my grandson, Dwayne Tolbert McGhee- Muhammad who was murdered. You will be home sooner, than later now that you know the power of manifesting. Akbar Muhammad, you will forever be in my heart. Imani Muhammad, my Princess may your college experience grant you peace, and success. To my great-grandchildren, Darelle Muhammad Jr, Nyla Muhammad, and D'asia Muhammad, each one of you are the reason for this legacy asset so that each one of you can share this legacy asset with your children's, children, children, and their children's children to have and to hold for their lifetime.

May Allah grant you the abundance of peace, blessings of health and prosperity. You are Muhammad. Worthy to be praised. Praised worthy much!

Shirley Muhammad is the owner of Your Professional Tax & Accounting Services, where she has been the senior tax accountant the past 23 years. She was born in Pittsburgh, Pennsylvania where she currently resigns. Ms. Muhammad graduated from Westinghouse High School, a public school located in Pittsburgh, PA. She graduated from Duquesne University also located in Pittsburgh, Pennsylvania where she received a bachelor's degree in sociological research and journalism. She later received a master's degree in accountancy from the University of Phoenix. She has been employed as an accountant for both city of Pittsburgh and Allegheny

County Controller's Offices. Ms. Muhammad publishes fictional short stories entitle Helpless. These are short stories dealing with forensic tax fraud. Ms. Muhammad was the consultant to an original play, A Nation Can Rise No Higher Than Its Woman,

She is an executive life coach where she helps individuals and teams to increase awareness, set up business goals and develop as leaders and influencers.

Ms. Muhammad's pride and joy is developing projects and programs for her nonprofit organization, Your Sister's Project, Inc. She also enjoys walking and taking photographs in nature.

She is a graduate of CORO Women in Leadership Class 8. Ms. Muhammad was selected in the 2008 New Pittsburgh Courier 50 Women of Excellence Award in Business.

EUGENE POOLE

ALWAYS STRIVE TO LIVE YOUR LIFE SO THAT YOU CAN HELP OTHERS

When I was a child, I was always looking for something that made sense of why I was here and what I was supposed to do. I remember when I was two years old growing up in the Bronx River Housing Projects in New York City my older sister asked me to give her my milk bottle. Although I wasn't quite sure why she needed it, I knew she was my older sister whom I adored and love even now, I gave her my bottle. After all, she was a year older than me. After thanking me for handing over my bottle, she would hide behind the door from my mother and drink all my milk. Afterwards, she would give me back my empty bottle. Once I put the bottle back in my mouth and realized that there was no more milk I would cry loudly, and my mother would come to see why I was crying because she knew she had just given me a full bottle of warm milk. Since my mother was upset and my stomach was empty it made me wonder why I did not know that my sister would drink my milk.

As I got older, I realized that I needed to find a way to understand why I was here and what I was supposed to do. Although I never felt poor, I knew there were times in the week when food would become scarce until my father got paid on Fridays because my mother did not work outside of our home. My Parents had five children, three girls and two boys. My sister, who used to drink my milk, was the oldest girl, and I was the oldest boy. As time went on, we were introduced to the Lutheran Church where their members would come into our housing Projects singing and preaching the Gospel on the streets. We would all gather round to see what they were singing about. Once they piqued our interest, they invited us to join their church. Their approach was much appreciated because although there were other churches in the area, we were never approached or invited by any of the other churches

One of the greatest gifts provided by this church was their encouragement of everyone to be born again. They also had us studying Scripture and teaching us how to apply the Scripture passages in our daily lives. As young teenagers we attended weekly Bible study sessions and continued to learn how to address and overcome challenges in our daily living as young adults. They specifically addressed issues regarding life choices and personal responsibility. They taught the importance of not following the crowd and standing up for our faith. Although I knew I was not a perfect human being, I strongly felt the need to strive for better behavior and take personal responsibility for living a life that would encourage others to follow Christ. Although striving to live a better life and encouraging our neighbors to do likewise, it was extremely challenging because it addressed the two basic questions I had wondered about as a child. Why I was here, and what I was supposed to do.

The more I studied and read Scripture passages, I finally began to understand that I was here to love, trust, and serve our God. In addition, I had an obligation to share the good news of salvation so that others might be saved and enjoy God's grace, goodness, and mercy. Although I knew that this was a tall order, I fully embraced it and gave my first sermon in my church, Abiding Presence, at the age of 14. I was excited and fulfilled because I had finally found a reliable way to study life and gained better insight, and wisdom regarding the ways of the world. Living in New York City forced me to grow up whether I was ready or not. The threat of bullying, gangs, drug addiction, and a host of other challenges were always at our doorsteps. Therefore, I had to decide every day what or who I would follow. If I was not firm in my beliefs, there were always numerous opponents who were willing to discourage me from my journey.

Sometimes, our life or the life of our family members would be put at risk for our decisions. I had to lift weights and learn self-defense by studying Judo and Karate so our opponents would know that we were willing to defend ourselves, if necessary. I knew early on that my decision would not be for the faint of heart because the history of Christianity is filled with stories of how so many Saints were tortured and killed over the centuries for the sake of their Christian faith. Therefore, I knew that I would not be the first to sacrifice my life for the sake of the faith.

Given the historical facts of the Christian Church, and my personal experience with being born again on December 8, 1963, which was one week before my 14th birthday, I had transitioned into a new person. I knew I had been changed from that point and no one could convince me otherwise. Therefore, my conversion to the faith with Jesus Christ as my personal Lord and savior, would be the first person, after my parents, who influenced my life because Jesus taught us how and why we must live together in peace and harmony throughout the World.

My favorite quote is in the book of Proverbs, from that, the New American Bible. Revised Edition 2011. Proverbs 1 Verse 7: "Fear of the Lord is the beginning of knowledge; fools despise wisdom and discipline". If anyone wants to learn about life and the pursuit of Wisdom, I encourage them to read the book of Proverbs daily because it provides instructions and wisdom on how to conduct one's life. It will not disappoint you and you will be wiser for its exhortations and lessons.

PARENTS

I thank God every day for the wonderful parents he gave me. My parents loved their children and we loved them right back. Although our parents were loving, they also knew they had a tremendous responsibility to raise us by teaching us right from wrong, and for us to get a good education. We had to attend both school and church consistently. In addition, there were friends and relatives of our parents who felt an obligation to inform our parents if they saw us doing anything that was not in line with our parents' beliefs and practices. Baby Boomer children were taught to respect their Elders, especially in the African American Community.

Although my parents did not have much formal education, they still encouraged us to get a good education. My Mother had a 12th grade education, and my father had a 6th grade education because he grew up on an African American family farm in Alabama where he had to work the fields and bring in the crops. In those days the boys always had to work the fields but many of the girls were sent for higher education. That was the case with my father's sister because she became a Medical Technician and moved to live in a high-rise Co-Operative known as Esplanade Gardens that was designed for moderate to middle income families in Harlem, New York. My Aunt also worked at Harlem Hospital that was not far from Esplanade Gardens.

Despite the difference between my father and my paternal Aunt's economic circumstances, we were all very close. My mother used to baby sit my aunt's daughter while my aunt worked at the hospital. It was a mutually beneficial family arrangement where everyone prospered. We were also particularly close during the major holidays of Thanksgiving and Christmas. We had a lot of fun and encouragement from our famil members, and close friends. Everyone seemed to bake and share their goodies with each other, and with those who did not have much to eat. There was no stigma that I could detect just because someone did not have enough to eat because we were used to sharing with our neighbors. In fact, I remember when my father would go fishing with his friends in Upstate New York they would often catch so many fish that no one could store all the fish in their refrigerators so that the fish would not spoil. As a result, my father would knock on the doors of neighbors who could store and consume the extra fish and offer the fish to them free of charge. My father would be extremely happy when the neighbors accepted the fish because he knew that the fish would not be wasted and that he provided food to his good neighbors in friendship and encouragement. I do not think many people today appreciate how far good will goes when it is done in love with the right attitude. Good will in the neighborhood has a ripple effect that can last many years into the future. You never know where your blessings will go and when they will come back to you. Since my father had always shared his good fortune with hunting and fishing bounties with his neighbors, his reputation and our family's reputation for doing good deeds helping our neighbors grew into tremendous love and respect for our family. Our neighborhood also developed a deep sense of loyalty to each other. As children, if we saw any of our parents in the neighborhood needing help carrying groceries or any other type of help, we gladly assisted them.

The sense of good will, respect and love even extended to those who were not always doing the right things. If someone was doing something wrong and they knew us, they would not attack or rob us simply because they knew us or knew of our reputation for doing good. This brings me to my mother and her best friend. As I grew up and moved away from the neighborhood, things began to change for the worst. As more and more children were growing up without one or none of their parents, a drug epidemic began. More children were getting hooked on drugs and the Clinton Administration began to crack down on crime. Unfortunately, many young college-age African American children who were found with a certain amount of Marijuana began to receive long prison sentences, while those in the white community that were convicted of offenses with cocaine received much lighter sentences and received help for their addictions. Most people realize 20 years later that many of the sentencing guidelines were biased against African Americans and other minorities. Most of these black and minority offenders admittedly should have been drug treatment programs as well. Therefore, the children of these minority families were thrown into a system that did not address their emotional and financial needs. As a result, our streets became even more dangerous with drug addicted children who were robbing and hurting everyone out of a desperation to get high or find their next meal.

My mother and her best friend were concerned senior citizens who wanted to find a way to help these young folks. My mom was also the victim of one of these young people who stole her pocketbook and went on a spending spree with her credit cards. However, my mother was able repay them with kindness. She decided that since these children were also very hungry, she began distributing paper plates with food after church. She and her best friend became the Dynamic Duo distributing food and chocolate cake to those who were living on the street. My mom's chocolate cake could tame anger in most people, especially me. As my mom and her best friend continued helping complete strangers who were desperate for a little food, a kind word, or a blanket, they became well known throughout the community. However, one day, one of the desperate souls who did not know my mom decided to rob her. To my mom's surprise, the community members who were also living on the streets, came to my mothers' rescue and told the other would-be robber that they could not rob their mother. If they did, everyone was willing to protect my mom. The robber backed off and never tried to attack my mom again. My mother and her best friend had become the surrogate mothers to these young people who were living on the streets. My mother's free chocolate cakes were well known, and she began receiving orders from people who wanted to purchase a piece of her chocolate cake. Some people even purchased whole cakes. My mom did not really know what to charge them because she had given so much to the community at no charge. Therefore, she would just accept any donation to keep purchasing more flour and chocolate.

One of the best things about my parents is that they always encouraged us to do our best. No matter how rich or poor you are, you should always encourage your kids. When I was five years old, I began observing adult behavior. One of the things that had a tremendous impact on my thoughts as a child was the difference between those who told the truth and those who told lies. I realized that those who told lies, had bad things follow them. I saw the disappointment and anger that lies had caused between adults, even if they loved each other. Therefore, I turned my attention to observing my parents. I noticed one consistent thing about my parents and their relationship with me. They did not lie to each other and would not lie to me. If my father said he was going to do something on Friday, he did it. His word was as good as gold. My mom did the same with my father. Therefore, I knew that I could believe in my parents and trust them. They were equally effective when they were praising or punishing me. I could count on them carry out their pledge whether it was positive or negative. I quickly learned that 'no' was 'no', and 'yes' was 'yes', even if I tried to get one of them to say, 'yes' and the other said 'no'. They did not contradict each other. Now I knew that whatever either of them said, that was the gospel truth, and there was no need to try to go between them.

Now that I knew that my parents did not lie and that I could take their word as the gospel truth I asked them if they thought I could do one of my school tasks. My mom said: 'Eugene, you could do anything that you set your mind to do'. Wow! This was a drop the mike moment for me. My mother just told me that I could do anything that I set my mind to do. In addition, since I knew that my mother did not lie, I believed I could do it no matter what anyone else had to say. Once my mother told me that, I believed it hook, line, and sinker. Therefore, I went out on my mission in this world to accomplish something great. It didn't matter if it took some time to achieve it. I just knew in my heart that I was going to do something great, and my mind was made up because MOM said I could do it. This why I say that parents should always encourage their children no matter what anyone else says. Parents can light a fire of desire for achievement that can last a lifetime. The other encouraging aspect for me is that my parents believed in me before I believed in myself. Seven decades later that fire of desire for achievement is still shining brightly today. As a result, I have two Master's degrees, with a host of certifications and achievements that will last me for the rest of my life. Therefore, always encourage your children, even if you are not certain because they may achieve things beyond your understanding or imagination. Read to your children, especially bedtime stories. Get them involved with music and other group activities, because they will learn how to work well with others and build their tolerance levels and social skills. Try to attend their events as much as possible. Good parenting with boundaries can develop the right type of skills and discipline required for years to come.

Although my parents had limited formal education my siblings and I achieved much more with 2 out of five graduating college with 2 Master's degrees for myself. My wife and I have traveled the world and ran major projects for the US Government and Industry. No one would have imagined at the time that we would come so far from such humble beginnings. However, it happened during my parents' lifetime, and we are grateful to God for all His blessings. Therefore, we will continue to keep our faith and find more ways to pay it forward by being a blessing to those who have yet to be born.

Therefore, we encourage everyone to keep reading Scripture and apply it to their life. Be kind to each other by walking in each other's shoes. Always encourage your children to do their best. We must foster the same love and respect for children who have lost their parents due to war, incarceration, or any other circumstance that may not develop their sense of love for themselves and others. We must not neglect the poor and the needy because it illustrates the strength of our Nation. We should not be quick to judge others.

As a final thought I want to thank my wife, Freddie Mae for encouraging me to get my Master's degree, and to continue working on behalf of others. My wife serves as a great inspiration to me because although she has achieved much as a leader in her scientific and academic pursuits, she is always willing to reach back to show others how to achieve the same results. She is a true servant leader who is always willing to help others without expecting anything in return; including helping me edit this manuscript. I will always be thankful to my wife for her love, support, and 42 wonderful years of marriage.

Eugene Poole was born, educated, and raised in the Bronx, New York City. He majored in Biology and graduated with a B.A. in Biology from Concordia College in Moorhead, Minnesota. He also received a Dual Masters from the University of Maryland Global Campus (UMGC) with an MBA and a second Masters in Cybersecurity Policy. He has a certification in the Affordable Care Act (ACA) from the National Association of Health Underwriters (NAHU) and is a Certified Project Manager (PMP) granted by the Project Management Institute (PMI). Eugene also has life and health insurance licenses in 20 States, and serves as the CEO of his own health insurance agency listed as the Aligned Benefits Group, Inc.

Eugene resides in Upper Marlboro, Maryland with his wife and family. His favorite quote is in the book of Proverbs, from the New American Bible. Revised Edition 2011. Proverbs 1 Verse 7: "Fear of the Lord is the beginning of knowledge; fools despise wisdom and discipline".

JENNEH BROOKS

WHO INFLUENCES ME?

There are several women with whom I have associated myself that have been of the greatest influence in my life. I can count the number of influential women who contributed to my development into womanhood. I was influenced both positively and negatively by these women, whether they were good or bad, whether they were known or unknown, contrite things that were deemed as both positive and negative influences. Having these influencers in my life, assisted me to develop this woman I am today, and without each of their contributions, I cannot possibly imagine what my life experiences would have been like.

The first person who transformed my life for the positive was my eldest sister Elaine Brooks. I met Elaine at two-years-old before my mother's untimely death. My mother went to my father's home to seek financial support, but he wasn't there, and so, "this is what I was told."

Upon her arrival, my sister informed my mother that my father was away, so my eldest sister offered to keep me overnight until the return of my father. Our mother said she would come back the following week when he returned. On her way back home to her village my mom was killed in a fatal vehicular accident, never to be seen again, and at some point during my early years of life, my sister Elaine left to come to the United States. I was left in the care of my step-mother and other siblings and I can only be grateful for the blessings I received, since my sister offered for me to stay with her or else it would have been two fatal losses instead.

Because of my mother's demise, I had to learn at an early age to become less emotional and more focused on how to survive living with 15-20 other siblings, but how was I able to do that at such a tender age? Those people, despite being my blood relatives were strangers to me. My mother was gone and my father was not someone with whom I was familiar, and I was no longer in the care of my mother so, I had to learn quickly how to fit in. This instant transition led me to my stepmother, my father's wife who had only one child for my father, and their child passed away at the early age of 13-years-old. I quickly learned he had several other children. As time passed, I became part of this family and I had to earn my way if I was to be viewed as a dignified person rather than a freeloader.

My stepmother, Caroline Washington-Brooks was a tough cookie. One thing Ma (is what we call her) had, was zero tolerance, when it came to addressing our older siblings by their first name. I quickly learned she was the head of her household, and everyone had to follow the rules of her home. Cleanliness was one of the rules with no option, so I did what I was told, having no choice but to comply. I quietly did so and kept my head down and my emotions to myself. Learning early that what I felt was secondary to what others wanted me to feel. I spent years under the tutelage of my stepmom and I am honestly grateful for the harsh lessons learned now. She taught me homemaking skills, cooking skills, sewing skills and my personal lessons on becoming a lady. Of course, the latter was not taught, it was inferred from what was not expected or nor acceptable.

After my father's death in 1982, my sister Elaine brought me into this country when I was 10 years old. When I was lived in Liberia, I was moved from home to home, however. I am very grateful to Sister Elaine for saving my life, because if it wasn't for her, I would've been killed along with my mother, and the opportunity to leave Liberia was beyond me.

Among the things I am most grateful for is the right to pursue an education in America, because living in Liberia, I doubt I would have been able to receive an education. During my youth I was in and out of school and I am not sure an education would have been possible for me during that time. The county had just been immersed in a civil war that caused the lives of thousands of people, and many villages were wiped out entirely. In fact, I didn't know anyone from my mother's family whether they were dead or alive, nor where my mother's grave site is, nor a picture of her and what she looks like.

I am so thankful for Sis. Elaine who graciously put a roof over my head and clothes on my back and made sure I was safe. Because of her, I got the opportunity to meet another sister Miatta Brooks-Hoff, and through Miatta I got to meet another wonderful Sister Theresa Brooks. Sis. Miatta's strongest character was her ambition and I admired Miatta's desire to enjoy success in America. She was beautiful, friendly, strong and intelligent. Miatta told me stories of her dreams of going to college and becoming a successful person in the United States. She attended Kean College where she obtained a degree in Business Management.

Miatta transformed my life by giving me hope, and told me to stay focused, study hard and stay positive and that I could always count on her for life advice. She told me to be humble, speak only when spoken to and always keep God first, and so, I went to live with her after my fourteenth birthday. There she taught me many things, such as how to carry myself as a young woman and to live independently without anyone's control. Miatta said to me one day: "There is nothing more important in life than being a blessing in someone else's life." I could talk to her about anything, and she would come to Sister Elaine's home from time to time and I would always look forward to seeing her.

Sis. Miatta didn't have much at that time, but she shared what little she had with me. She introduced me to her mother's side of the family, and they treated Zsari and I like we were blood relatives and I feel like they are. Sis. Miatta's mother became my mother, which I called Ma-Musu. Her siblings, her aunt's, Sadutu Clarke, Jatu Kegley, and Munma Kemokai and all their children became my cousins. Sis. Miatta showed me love, something I've never had. She said, be kind to others because it will come back to you one day. She encouraged me to keep my opinions about people to myself, nor put anyone down, and that I shouldn't be satisfied with being mediocre. She further taught me not to get excited about anything which ultimately made me fearful of others' opinions of me, untrustworthy and more introverted. At that tender age, I was unaware that my life was being groomed for the woman I am today. Thankfully, the positive influencers outweighed the negativity I received during early childhood and I am eternally grateful for having a strong relationship with my sisters and with God. My life circumstances have always led me back to the source of my soul and of my very being and I will always be grateful for Sis. Miatta's unconditional love and guidance.

My best friend, Ms. Esther Tyndal has positively influenced my life for more than 38 years. Esther is a thoughtful, loving and very kind person, although if you had met her, this would not be your first impression when meeting her due to her serious demeanor. Esther has helped me in so many ways, and as young as she was, she was way ahead of me in her thinking and beliefs, for she was bright and very intelligent for her age. She has such a beautiful smile that would bring many, many souls to their knees. Esther graduated from Seton Hall University with a bachelor's degree and immediately returned to schooling at Fordham University where she earned her master's degree--both of Esther's degrees are in social work.

Esther always has time to help anyone in need, especially the elderly in the community, patiently teaching them how to use the computer, taking them to their doctor appointments or even spending money out of her own pocket to buy food for those in need. I am also a recipient of her kindness when I was in desperate need. She is the kind of woman who will take the shoes off her feet and clothes off her back and give them to you while she is in the snow. I didn't know then that all these things Esther was doing helped forge her character and led her to her calling of becoming a social worker.

Let her tell it, despite going to nursing school and almost completing her course studies, she became discouraged and walked away, and it was years later, when she decided to return to complete her nursing degree and was denied entry and decided to take a class in the human service field. There, she fell in love with the idea of becoming a social worker, and one day, she said, "I chose nursing, but social work chose me and things have been effortless in my life since". When I look back over my life, I now come to realize and understand that this was truly Esther's calling because she had a compassionate heart to help others.

Well, let me take you on my journey through our childhood. I was about 12-year- old when I met Esther but sadly, friendship between Esther and I was forbidden from the very start, because she had come from a well off family. One day, I saw her as she was putting out the trash in her backyard, and she said, "Hi," and I replied, "hi" and she then proceeded to ask me about my accent. That's when I told her I was from Liberia and had recently moved into the neighborhood.

That was the extent of our interaction until sometime after my sister, Elaine introduced herself to Esther's parents. At some point, my sister was invited over for dinner with Esther's family and that was my first memory of meeting Esther and her family officially at a Thanksgiving dinner where my sister took over a delicious treat of baked turkey with wild rice stuffing. Esther would later tell me, "That day was sealed in her mind forever, because it was the only time she enjoyed eating turkey and wished never to have it any other way." You see, little did they know that I had a love of cooking

We were not allowed to go outside much, so engaging with our neighbors was not exactly welcomed especially since we were one of four black families in a community of whites. Indeed, and I believe we were the fourth black family in the neighborhood. After meeting Esther and her brother, Chris, her father made it clear that they were not encouraged to keep company with my family. We were *"seldom seen and less heard"* since their household was considered well-to-do.

Despite her father's wishes, Esther continued to be my friend, and since that time, she and I have remained and maintained a friendship of sisterhood for most of our adult lives. Over the years, I have watched her growth and determination to do something different, so she ignored the naysayers and focused on what was propelling us to be friends rather than what was being said against our friendship.

We both eventually moved out of our family's home and into our own place. I had to do that much sooner than I wanted, however, we remained in contact thanks to our bond and the friendship of our mutual friends who further kept us connected.

As I recall our trials and tribulations, I can only cite the many times we were each other's support and that caused us both to become successful in our own right. I always asked Esther for personal advice, and when you ask her for advice, she would ask you," How do you want it? Do you want the truth, or do you want me to sugarcoat it? She knew no other way to tell me exactly how she felt, although she was bold when I sometimes just needed her to listen. I never had to question her integrity, and I knew I would get the truth from her because she didn't have two tongues. Esther and I are just one year apart, and she helped me believe that my situation was only temporary and that one day I will look back and laugh about it. As a teenager, I didn't have much life experience. My self-esteem was always so low and I always called on her for help; to pick her brains, and this continues to this day, especially when I was going through some of the most difficult times in my life.

Everyone believes money is the answer to all your sorrows, however, let me be one of the first to tell you, "That is not the case". As well off as Esther's family was, it did not satisfy, nor fulfill all her yearnings and needs. I found out that we were both lacking in several areas and as "wounded beings," so we found commonality with one another as we sought the comfort of each other during our youth. We were going through similar issues, and it was during these times, we depended upon each other for emotional support. It was because of our strong minds that we were able to overcome our diversities and rise to the challenges that presented itself time after time.

We were unwilling to succumb and be defeated, and regardless of the frustrations and failures, we kept ourselves encouraged especially with keeping our eyes stayed on God. As a result of having a sound relationship with God, our peace was constantly tested; however, "His peace" became mine to remain focused. Esther quickly recognized, once out on her own, that the lessons of God created a stronghold in her life, and as a result of that, it gave me the momentum to look forward and work harder in spite of whatever hardship I was encountering at that time. As time rolled by, I tried to encourage myself in the same mindset. I credited my immediate success to surrounding myself and those who surrounded me, with having an open mind and being willing to be uncomfortable in order to get comfortable and further become successful.

She has such growth and a promising future and I further believe that her determination and unwillingness to settle for "NO" will bring her good fortune as she continues to explore new things and rise to new challenges. When you have a friend who not only has your back but speaks her truth, it's considered "Twice Blessed". Everything Esther has ever done for me has been nothing but extraordinary, beyond words, in fact I consider her one of my beloved sisters.

HOW ZSARI INFLUENCED ME

I have always dreamt of being a mother, so the days grew closer with just one month to go before Zsari's delivery. On May 2nd, 1997, I went to the hospital for my regular doctor checkup, not knowing that day would be the day she would be born. The nurse came in the room and said, "Ms. Brooks, you have been on the stress test for hours and there is no movement. We are concerned, the doctor will be in a few minutes to pull amniotic fluid from your stomach. The doctor confirmed that the test was necessary because there was no movement. It was necessary to run this test to make sure your baby is doing ok." I waited about 30 minutes, then the nurse came back into the room and said,

"Ms. Brooks, we may have to induce you right away, because your daughter isn't breathing and so, three-and- a-half hours later she was born, and they hurriedly took her away.

The day had finally arrived for her delivery, but I didn't get to meet her, because after giving birth, she was suddenly whisked away because she wasn't breathing. Although I was very worried, I knew she was a fighter, and so, I kept asking the nurse what was going on. All she would say is that she's going to be ok and so, two days had passed and I didn't get to see my baby girl. On the third day the nurse came into my room and said my baby had drank a full bottle of pedialyte and that Zsari had the lungs of an opera singer. Two hours later, I finally got to meet her, my little seven pounds, five ounces little girl. She was just perfect for me and if I never have any more children again, I was so grateful to God for her.

Zsari is like my best friend, and not to be taken lightly, though, I am still her mother. She has played a major part in my life, and because of her coming into my life, I am a mother today. I never knew what true love felt like until I met her. You see, previously I had two miscarriages, each at five and half months. After my second miscarriage, I decided to give up, because the loss was very emotional and painful for me, but my plan wasn't God's plan. This pregnancy had lots of challenges for me. At four months, I had to have my cervix stitched up and was advised by my doctor to stay off my feet and during those four months, I had to keep my feet propped at a 90 degrees to hold her in. I was only allowed to go to the restroom and to meet my doctor's appointment. She would sleep all day and move around my belly at night. "Her father's affectionately nicknamed me "Vampire". Zsari was determined to be here and so since she came into my life, she has been nothing but an inspiration for me. As she grew up, I noticed how she used to mimic me a lot, from how I walked, made my bed, and how I cooked. She used to say she wasn't going to be like me in the way that I loved doing various crafts and DIY projects, that's exactly how she came to be. I am so happy and inspired by her determination and love for creativity.

Zsari is a shy introvert and is a very talented dancer. I watch her personality develop over the years and her determination, work ethic and her courage to become an entrepreneur to make something of herself. My relationship with Zsari remains to be one of the most precious and cherished life has ever given me. She has never once disrespected me. She encourages me to be strong even though she's young and she would give advice.

She attended St. Andrew's Episcopal School from 6th - 12th grade and graduated in 2015 and received her high school diploma. She got her graduate degree studying television and radio with a minor in Communication Management and Design; graduating in 2019. She is currently attending American University studying Marketing, and will graduate this year in 2022. She aspires to create a space for friends and colleagues to express themselves, and her ambition keeps her going. I know she will be a success and I am so proud of her achievements.

***

I want to dedicate this to my family, and to my parents: Mom, Miatta Zodua and Dad Uriah T. J. Brooks. Thank you for giving me life, and rest in perfect peace. Thanks to my step-mothers: Caroline Washington-Brooks and Musu Kemokai. Thanks to all my sisters, especially Elaine Brooks for saving my life and for giving me hope for the future, and to Miatta Brooks-Hoff, Theresa Brooks, Genevieve Brooks, Angie Brooks and Esther Tyndall. I also dedicate this to my brothers, Chris Brooks, Roland Hoff, Thomas Benson, Bai Benson, Lahai Swaray, Victor Brooks, Urias Brooks.

Thanks to all my aunts: Sadatu Clarke, Jatu Kegley, Bendu Fahnbulleh, Siatta Sandimanie, and to my Uncles. Peter Clarke and Willie Kegle. To my cousins: Jojo Iaac, Marilyn Sawyer, Foudiya Henri, Ralph Henri, Patricia Kamara, Chris Henri, Martee Henri, Angel McLean-Freeman. To my nieces: Gamelia Milton, Laberta Jenkins, Romitta Hoff, Allen Mawola, Tenneh Sandimanie, Brianna McLean, Cameron Brooks, Lilly Tyndall.

To my nephews: Ellington Brooks, Urias Brooks, Justin Brooks, Lorenzo Hoff, Quincy Hoff, Tumi Tyndall. To my friends: Lois Harris, Tanya Young, Ralph Henderson, Patricia Henderson, Lark Daniel, Ramona Jones, Elisabeth Babatunde, Carol Boyd, Eddie Boyd, Tina Panye, Michelle Walker-Davis, Lincoln Haley, Shurliana Haley.

I am everlastingly grateful to the Almighty God for giving me an extraordinary family and friends. Thank you all for sharing your life with me and loving me just as I am.

Jenneh Brooks was born in Liberia and migrated to the United States at the age of ten. She is very passionate about helping people who are in need and encourages others to help the less fortunate. "No one knows what the future holds." She is inspired by her better half, Stanley Matthews. Stan, "Thank you for all that you have helped me to accomplish, for I am eternally grateful," and. to my daughter Zsari and step-son Elijah, thanks for loving me just as I am.

MARY SYMMONDS

LIFE'S LESSONS

The history of man is replete with stories of people who have come into our lives and influenced us in different ways, imperceptibly most of the time. Unaware, we take actions or make choices on our life's path based on values we have inculcated.

We are not responsible for our station in life. I come from a middle class family of six children. My mother was a trained nurse turned housewife and my father was an educator, parliamentarian, and entrepreneur. Coming from a society founded on slavery my parents' paths to middle class were not automatic. No matter our station, we encounter challenges and my family history was not without its challenges.

I was born and grew up on a tiny Caribbean island, Barbados. Each of us has a story to tell about the people that influenced our trajectory. Many have influenced me. In this chapter I will share about the impact my mother, my second mother and my father had on my life. To them I am eternally grateful and through sharing these stories I hope to impact others.

My mother was the essence of Resilience, love, kindness, generosity, listening, gender empowerment and forgiveness.

My mother passed away when I had just turned 12. Though our interaction was brief, my mother has had an enduring impact on who I have become. Short and plump, she was barely 5 feet tall, while my father towered over her at 6 feet in height. Her heart was large enough to harbor love for all six of us and the people whose lives she touched. She exuded confidence, had a great sense of humor and had a hearty laugh which I inherited. My mother shaped my views on the role of women in society. She was born in 1911 and in her young adult years even as women continued to struggle for equality, laws were put in place which prohibited married women from working. Though she was a qualified nurse, she became a housewife on marriage. I saw from the many other women around me that contributed to my life and development the degree of sacrifice that qualified women of my mother's generation made when they had to give up work outside the home. Housework and child rearing are indeed demanding work but I recognized women also need to have their own self-expression through fulfilling on their talents. Society itself is denied of the vital contribution of women. I saw that it was necessary and possible to both pursue one's profession or vocation and raise a family. Thankfully as an adult I was able to create the support system I needed to play my role as nurturer and professional.

My mother also shaped my attitude towards gender roles very early in life. She made sure that all the siblings played a role in the household. Perhaps it was because she herself had six siblings, only one of whom was a brother. Perhaps her mother required the girls to "molly coddle" him, leaving him free of household responsibilities, shaping his expectations of women as this gender bias is prone to do. Although we had assistance in the home, she required that we made our own beds for example, not, as was common in that era, expecting the girls to play these roles for our brothers. Boys and girls helped set and clear the breakfast, lunch, and dinner table. My eldest brother combed my hair on occasion. When she did her Saturday baking, she involved both my brothers, my sister and me. I saw early on that there were roles that were common to both males and females. Although my brothers were given more freedom than us girls in terms of socializing, I grew up considering myself equal to my brothers as far as what was possible in my life was concerned.

I could see why my mother's chosen profession was nursing. She had an inimitable way of listening for what was important for others and for making us all feel special, qualities needed in a nurse. In my case, she knew I loved reading and encouraged that, making it possible for me to go to the public library weekly along with my little sister. As a mother myself I realize that responding the needs of children is important. Though my father discouraged movie going in preference for reading, my mother could see the value of different forms of entertainment and storytelling. She worked with us on drama and creative writing at home, making up plays in which she also played a role. She also took us to movies and encouraged my father to take us to the drive in for movies he would approve of.

My mother also saw that an important part of her life's role was being generous and giving back to those less fortunate than herself, contributing to redressing inequalities in a society divided by a history not of its making. She engaged in events that were organized by associations she was a member of, associated with her church as well as civic organizations. I was therefore schooled from an early age in the importance of civic responsibility. I see it as my duty to do my part to contribute to a society where everyone has access to a safe and comfortable life.

My mother came from a family of musicians. She also played the piano and instilled in us the importance of music in our lives, the calming effect on our mood, and music's contribution to our creativity. Thinking back, I recall her sitting at the piano to play. It occurs to me that that was her way of relaxing. Today we would call it today meditation. She ensured that we all learned to play an instrument and to value the importance of music in our lives.

She had an ability to see what was important to each of us and to nurture and encourage it. My two sisters were interested in nursing and my mother shared with them what it was like to be a nurse. It is not surprising that they decided to pursue that profession. My youngest sister was very athletic. She loved swimming and my mother encouraged and permitted this. She became a star tennis player and coach. This listening capacity

I took into my life. I realized that being able to listen for and nurture the strengths of people around us is the essence of leadership. Identifying and encouraging the contribution of everyone in one's team is a very important skill for increasing our effectiveness in life.

Another aspect of my mother's listening capability was her ability was to listen and respond without judgement. Over family dinner or Sunday family lunch there were discussions about occurrences in the society. I observed that my mother would not respond with judgement or say anything that was unkind. She also discouraged us from wallowing in the misfortunes of others or saying things that were unkind. Her maxim was "if you can't say something kind about someone, don't say anything". I thus learned early on that it was important to give everyone a fair chance and most of all not to gossip as gossip was harmful.

It was only later in life that I realized that from the time I was seven years old my mother had cancer. She travelled to the US for medical treatment where she underwent a mastectomy. She was nevertheless resilient. We were blessed that after her treatment she was in remission for four years. What I recall is her amazing energy and untiring spirit. She continued to play her role as, nurturer, mother, and social contributor, ensuring we had the guidance we needed, organizing our birthday parties, ensuring we did our homework, organizing our plays, listening to our concerns and challenges and those of others and contributing to philanthropic efforts. The lesson I took from all of this was not to let our circumstances get in the way of our actions.

My kind mother was also a strict disciplinarian. She did not tolerate disobedience and demanded respect. Once, when I was about 7 years old my mother combed my hair for school in a style I did not like. To my sister's consternation while en-route to school I unbraided my thick head of hair and had difficulty rebraiding it neatly. I arrived, unkempt, at my Anglican convent school run by nuns who expected obedience and decorum.

My punishment was writing lines and once home I was lectured and required to kneel in the corner for an hour. The humiliation was unspeakable, but I learned many lessons that day, including the need to act responsibly and to be accountable for my actions, and kindness should not be construed as weakness. Though my mother was kind, she was not to be taken as incapable of requiring discipline and accountability. That episode in vanity taught me that my actions have consequences

MY SECOND MOTHER: LOVE, KINDNESS, RESILIENCE, THRIFT

Following my mother's passing another figure that would have a lasting impact on my life was the lady who I would call my "second mother". She was a beautiful lady who resembled Lena Horn. She had the kindest heart. When my mother passed away, she was there for me. Her daughter was my best friend and had a heart as big as her mother's so they both embraced me. I learned from the age of 12 that I should always be there for people in need especially when they are in their lowest moments, treating them with love and kindness. In my international career I made my home open to anyone in need and still do. My sister used to say, in a kind way, "You pick up all the strays". I have learned to create "family" wherever I am and to make others feel at home and be a contribution to others whenever there is a need.

My "second mother" being younger than my mother, the legal framework that impacted her had changed so that she was able to practice her own profession. She was an entrepreneur. I admired her strength, and this reinforced the views I was shaping about gender roles, my own aspirations, goals, and values; values I pass on to my son and daughter and to other young people about gender equality. Namely, both men and women have a role to play in our society. Denying 50 percent of our population the right to contribute to our society diminishes our ability to transform our societies. We therefore need to raise our children to respect the complementary roles men and women play. In my marriage my husband and I shared the nurturing and child rearing roles in concert with our professional or occupational roles. As professionals we both had to ensure our children's needs were met and seamlessly shared our obligation to respond to the concomitant demands of child rearing and our schedules without making our children feel deprived.

I also learned the lesson of resilience from my second mother. She went through a heartbreaking divorce. By then I was an adult but I was devastated, as my friend's father was also a "second father" to me. I can only imagine what it was like for her. She however continued to be her cheerful, wise, and giving self. What she demonstrated was our ability as human beings to bounce back and move forward no matter the circumstances life presents. Our circumstances should not govern how we make steps forward in our lives.

This resilient, loving, generous woman also taught me another lesson; namely, the importance of women saving and making early investments. Through her I learned the importance of women being thrifty and making an investment in property ownership. She ran her own business and was able to set aside savings to obtain the financing to build a house which she was able to rent and have residual income. She used to tell me, "This is my pension". She said this at a time when she was still married. I can only imagine what her life would have been if she had not made that investment before the dissolution of her marriage.

MY FATHER:
PURPOSE, RESILIENCE, KINDNESS, THRIFT, AND FORGIVENESS

If you told me my purpose in life would have been defined by my father, I would have vehemently protested. To understand this statement, it is necessary to share the perception I had of my father until, as a young professional, I read about him just before his death.

I was one of a second batch of children, there being a 10 and 11 year gap between me and my elder siblings. Being the daughter of an ultra-conservative father from a different generation than the fathers of most of my peers caused clashes in expectations.

My father was always impeccably dressed. Seven days a week, he wore a suit and tie, well-polished shoes and a fedora hat. Unlike the fathers of my peers, he rarely wore casual clothing. I found this perplexing and embarrassing.

My father was an antique. Born in 1905, for special national events he wore a top hat and a waistcoat and tails. I remember with amusement my father wearing a blue one-piece swimsuit for men of an earlier era – like the type we see in black and white silent films, in contrast to other topless males. So considering his busy life and unavailability, his being a strict disciplinarian and conservative, I made my mind up that I did not like him. I also judged other aspects of his life, including his making my mother unhappy due to being unfaithful to her.

I so resented him that I did not invite him to my wedding. One of my aunts ensured he attended. In his wedding speech he said, "Despite the iconoclastic tendencies of our times, I am pleased to be present at the wedding of my beloved daughter…" At the time I resented that speech but later regretted rejecting him.

One of the first lessons I learnt from my father, was the importance of education.

In the era in which I grew up we had access to universal free primary and secondary education. While I was in secondary, or high school as it is known in the United States, free University was introduced. By contrast, in my father's era in the early 20th century, education for children of color was limited to elementary school with a school leaving age of 14. By the early 20th century the country had however achieved a high degree of mass primary or elementary schooling , but most black children did not attend secondary schools. Those who did won highly contested scholarships, insufficient to accommodate the abundant numbers of bright, eligible students. The abundant supply of talented students became pupil teachers at the schools they attended, eventually becoming teachers themselves. My father followed this path, contributing to the high standard of education for which the country became known. Teaching was his first professional occupation.

My father valued education and was renowned as an outstanding teacher. Many of his students went on to higher education as opportunities for education opened up. I inculcated the notion of the transformative value of education and its contribution to lifelong learning and knowledge acquisition. My father's life trajectory was a testament to that lifelong learning, regardless of our stage in life is important. This is particularly relevant in our era where the world of work is constantly evolving, calling on us to be adaptable and be able to acquire new skills to respond to changing demands. Although he was not physically present, we knew what was expected of us.

MY FATHER THE SELF-MADE MAN, PROPELLED BY PURPOSE.

My father was born just after a period in history when many self-made people in the United States had emerged. ; people like Booker T Washington born in 1837and Adam Carnegie born in 1835, and the famous black American female entrepreneur Madame C.J. Walker, born in 1867. These men and women emphasized the importance of having a work ethic, and can-do attitude and willingness to take risks. I imagine my father, an avid reader, was likely influenced by the stories of these and other fabled entrepreneurs. He himself lived to those important adages.

Carnegie also had a quality that I recognized in my father years later, a person who had a strong sense of social responsibility which defined his purpose.

There are no original ideas, just the courage to implement them. Carnegie is known for saying "A penny saved is a penny earned" ; my father implemented this. The newspaper article reported that he created the first black bank. He did this in an era when there was an astounding level of poverty among the bulk of the population of color and where, like in the US, the working class was exploited. Punitive laws prohibited movement to areas where higher wages could be earned, if violated, they led to imprisonment. There was also compulsory child labor for poor children. The laws of the day and the earning potential made property ownership a mere dream for the middle and working classes.

The bank enabled the poor to save, educate their children and acquire property. It encouraged savings among the working class who had no access to commercial banks which catered to the plutocracy and mercantile segments of the society. Its policy was that "No savings were too small".

While it ultimately failed due to competition with commercial banks which caused major shareholders, including him, to lose their investment, it was held up as an empowering example for which he received national honors. He said that he could have lived a private life and made millions based on the ideas he had, but he wanted to bring about improvements in the living conditions for future generations. He described it as the purpose given to him by his creator and he would do it all over again.

FORGIVENESS AND PURPOSE

After living my formative years not understanding and distancing myself from my father, I learned that his work was his legacy to me and others. I learned who he really was and the most important lesson of my life: That we all need to be connected to our life's purpose. I also learned forgiveness of myself and others for none of us are perfect. Through pursuing our purpose , life is not hard work. In the words of George Bernard Shaw:

"This is the true joy of life, the being used for a purpose recognized by yourself as a mighty one

I want to be thoroughly used up when I die, for the harder I work, the more I live."

Mary Symmonds is a retired United Nations Executive and International Economic and Social Development Practitioner. She is also the founder of The Global Leadership Coalition which builds socially responsible, ethical, entrepreneurial young male and female leaders between the ages of 18 and 29. Mary is a contributing Author to Amazon Best Seller, The Art of Resilience, Phoenixes Rising curated by Dr. Joy T. Vaughan. She is also the MBN Regional Chair for Africa.

SHIRROD LE'DET

THE RIGHT INFLUENCE
AT THE RIGHT TIME

Positive influence is the impact you have on other people or yourself by pointing out the strengths and virtues of others. Three have had such a positive influence on my life. These positive influences led to me transforming my life at pivotal times in both my life and career.

I had recently lost my job and I was working at my church full time. I was literally back to square one again with my life after being fired from a fifteen-year career. Oh yeah, did I mention married, a newborn and a 10-year-old daughter? Oh yeah, life was fantastic! I remembered that one of the ideas suggested was to go back to school and get my master's degree. My pastor was a big proponent of education, as well as a big supporter of taking full advantage of opportunities when they presented themselves. So, I figured why not since I had the time and in my current situation, it was the optimal idea to better myself, as that could position me for a better opportunity later.

I applied to Sullivan University, a local college where I received my undergraduate degree in Information Technology. Since it was a small, nearby institution, I already knew most of the faculty there, so to me it seemed logical to enroll there. I submitted my application with all supporting documentation, and received an acceptance within weeks. A few weeks went by, and then it was time to start classes, and so, I received my financial aid, which let's face it, is always the best part about college right? Yeah right, I was still trying to figure out the logic behind that decision. You know how people say it is all about timing. Well, I found this to be true with this experience, as for me the time was not now. I was not ready and it did not work out.

Having someone to encourage, motivate, and cheer you on can make all the difference in your life, and your success. Also, having someone who is willing to regularly check in on you, and ask how things are going, is such a wonderful way to impact the lives of other people and Torrey Woods is that individual who you would see always offering his services. He truly had a servant's heart and used it to serve God and others, which we would call servant leadership.

I recalled having a conversation with Torrey about getting my degree and finding the right program for me from this experience. It was during this time that I would find out who Torrey and Kim Woods were, but I wasn't ready for the impact and influence they would have on my life. Torrey would always ask the right questions and get me to do the inner work required to identify the specific insight to reach the best possible outcome. Through various conversations and research, I later applied, and was accepted to the Jack Welch Management Institute at Strayer University. This was a new Executive Master of Business Administration degree that was developed by the late Jack Welch. This program seemed tailored-made just for me. Torrey and Kim both were very supportive and excited for this opportunity for me. I contribute my success in completing the program with honors because of the support of many, but Torrey and Kim specifically.

Positive influences can help a person become better today than they were yesterday, because positive influence builds optimistic, affirmative, and constructive participation between both individuals in the relationship. Influencers are always dedicated to what makes and brings meaning to their lives, because they are a small portion of the population that believes in a life of purpose and goal-setting. Torrey and Kim Woods demonstrated this God-believing and purpose-focused life as individuals but also as husband and wife. They were a breath of fresh air to be around, and they lived the principles they would share and pour into me, and others. Every conversation that took place with either Torrey or Kim was from a place of willingness to help however they could. They were always ready to help those in need, never looking down on anyone or never asking for anything in return. They would express the same energy to help and serve with every encounter.

Influence is the power to have an important effect on someone or even something. If someone influences someone else, they are changing that individual or thing in an indirect but significant way. Sometimes a person who influences another does not intend to have any effect, but sometimes they are using influence to benefit themselves. Torrey and Kim Woods gave special attention to sharing and pouring into me about life, leadership, and being a spiritual covering for my family. Torrey mentored me in the areas of being a husband and father. These two were very instrumental in my development and growth as I began to identify another level of passion for leadership and business. They both had great experience in both of these areas, and would find every opportunity to coach and mentor me as I walked into this new chapter of my life.

One of the roles and responsibilities of our parents is to be the type of influence that helps to shape us into contributing citizens of society. Whatever that means, right? No seriously, our first examples and influences are that of our parents, so, therefore, it should be no surprise that my mother is one of those top influential people in my life. Now, for the record, my dad is just as much as a part of who I am today as she is, but there is a reason her influence was the greatest.

As parents, we influence our child's basic values, like religious values, and issues related to their future, such as making sound educational choices. The stronger our relationship with our child, the more influence we will have, because our children will be more likely to seek our guidance and value our opinions and support. My parents have always shown nothing but strength through even the worst of adversities that any relationship can even endure. It is amazing how things we think are meant to be to our detriment, actually work in the complete opposite direction and become a stepping-stone.

The reason my mother, Barbara Carter, is one of the three influences in my life is because of her continuous life example of putting God first in all things. WOW! Even as I write this, and see it in words, it is mind-blowing in terms of having the type of role model who truly loves and follows God with all her heart and soul. This is my mother. Yes, she carried me for nine months, and, yes, she gave birth to me, but then she gave me back to the one who gave me to her in the first place, God.

I am only seeing this revelation as I put these words on paper for you to read. There are many things we remember from our childhood—the good and bad. You know those moments where you were in trouble not because of what you did but for what your sibling did. I have plenty of those stories, as I'm sure we all do. My mom is one that really did not beat around the bush or tell half-truths; look, for her, it's either right or wrong and if you don't want to hear the answer then don't ask the question.

Now she may not agree with this but that's ok, it's my chapter, my perspective and perception, so I'm good. See how brave I am behind this keyboard, right now! What she would probably disagree with me about is that she is a disciplined person. Actually, I think I will go with dedicated, but disciplined, too. The way she lived her life and modeled the discipline of reading her Bible was amazing. I do not know how many Bibles she has or even how many she has gone through, but I know she was dedicated to making sure it was a part of her daily discipline. She was also a praying woman; now, did I see her pray every day as child growing up? The answer is no. But, the relationship between her and God that I witness today suggest that she knows Him and He knows her which tells me they talk all the time.

Do you ever ask yourself or wonder why some things happen the way they do or why opportunities present themselves out of nowhere, especially when you know that it had nothing to do with you or the intelligence that you think you have? Well, do you know that old saying that someone prayed for you? So, I attribute those times and opportunities to my mother talking to God on my behalf, as to me there is no other justification. Now, you would think that I am an only child but fortunately I am not; I am one of five. I know my mom prayed for us all equally and covered us daily or even hourly (just depending on what happened the previous week).

Parents are essentially the number one influencers in our lives, as their behavior greatly affects ours. They consciously and unconsciously instill their personal beliefs, opinions, ideas, and moral and ethical values in us that initially shapes our mindset. The way my mom demonstrated the dedication and discipline of prioritizing God has obviously had a major influence in my life, but you will be surprised to learn that I knew this only recently, like maybe over the past year or so. To give you context of the timeframe I mentioned, I am currently 42 years old (wide eye emoji). The purpose of this reference to age is that my mom's spiritual influence over my life took time, but did not have its full impact until I, too, had my own personal relationship with God.

Ok, I use to be slow too. So, once I had developed my own relationship with God, it was the discipline and dedication my mom modeled for me as a child and continues to model that has influenced the spiritual development and my relationship with God. To this day, no matter the conversation with my mom, there is always a reference to the Bible or a lesson learned through the orchestration of God. Whenever we are discussing or debating something (not too often do we really debate) but we always have this saying of "what is truth." When either of us bring this statement into the conversation, we know we mean, "What does the Bible say about it?" This shifts everything, and God has a great time, I believe, watching our little minds of knowledge go through this process of "truth." My mother has been a huge influence in my life but more specifically my spiritual growth and development; not by what she says, but how she lives.

As I complete this chapter with this last influence, the

relationships that transform my life, I wanted to reemphasize the definition of influence. It is the capacity to have an effect on the character, development, or behavior of someone or something, or the effect itself. This last individual is unique in their own right and has overcome and accomplished more than they ever thought possible. This last influencer has influenced me more than those mentioned and to date continues to have a tremendous impact. I am that person.

If you are wondering if this a joke, or a typo of some sort, it is not, because I am the person who has influenced the transformation of my life the greatest, and still does. Listen, one of the greatest challenges in life is influencing yourself in a world that constantly putting pressure on you to conform or assimilate to what they think you should be. This can be exhausting and even immobilizing. The reality is that someone will always be richer, prettier, smarter, stronger, younger, wiser, and possibly even funnier than you are. We face this paradox. Look, we are human and imperfect at that, so the more we influence ourselves to be ourselves, the more we can be enjoying life. Not to mention, reach greater levels of potential that ever thought possible.

Perfection is not what attracts people, authenticity does. To be influential to your own transformation you must grow your self-awareness, which is the conscious knowledge of one's own character, feelings, motives, and desires. When we are self-aware, we have the ability to recognize our talents and non-talents. Having this knowledge helps us to set and achieve goals that allow us to grow more organically into our authentic selves. Knowing our talents or strengths give us permission to feel confident in our own ability.

When I was first introduced to personal development, like really knowing and understanding the importance of it and its purpose, I became obsessed. I could not get enough of Les Brown, Eric Thomas, Norman Vincent Peale, Jim Rohn, Earl Nightingale, and so many more. Everything in my life started to transform. Why? I was not the same person when I finished reading, listening, or watching one of those aforementioned individuals. Let me be more specific, first I started to make peace with the uncontrollable things in my life. First, I figured out the things I could change and then changed them; and second, if I could not change something, then I learned to live with it. Wow, mind blowing, right? Not really, as we do this all the time, but are not consciously aware of it. What I learned is that if I change my attitude about the things I cannot control, I can then make peace with it. I have also learned that worrying about something is one of the worst techniques to solve problems.

I then figured out that I had to let go of the past, because, pointing out what others did wrong does not present any real gain for them, but I did this to myself daily. Instead of focusing on the lesson learned and making the necessary adjustments for the future, I was stuck in my past mistakes. We have to learn from our past and invest in the future by making the conscious decision to live for today. As part of my ability to influence myself and transform my life, I created a personal mission statement:

*"It's not about being right or wrong…
but being effective now, to experience the moment, to be
efficient in the future."*

Having this personal mission statement has allowed me to focus on what is important. What is important is discovering how I can make a difference in the many areas of my life, including leadership and community. What is important is not to live perfectly, which is impossible, but to live purposely. My core values are faith, family, impact, and abundance. Gaining self-awareness through personal development allowed me to have an influence and impact over my own self and life.

The last aspect of my own influence over myself was my understanding that I was worth the investment. See, I say that because what I am expressing is not a selfish act, but an action of self-care one. If I do not take care of me, then who will? Even more importantly, whose responsibility is it outside of myself? Right. Nobodies but mine; investing in me allows me to then, in turn, invest in others. Listen, I cannot give you what I do not have, and I cannot help you if I do not first help myself. Now here is the reality: investing in yourself might mean putting some money, time, and energy on the line to achieve the level of growth and personal development you are after. I know, because it cost me a lot. Fortunately, our own influence on our character development and behavior can be just as transformational as those from other positive influencers in our life. Never discount your own value and the power of influence you have, not only for those in your life, but for you as well.

***

I dedicate this chapter to you, my parents, Barbara and Curtis; without your encouragement, support and tough love, but love all the same, there is no telling how things could have turned out for me. I am forever grateful for you both. Torrey and Kim Woods, I pray that by reading this short chapter, you can see the value you both added to my life. Kim Woods, rest in peace my friend and mentor until we meet again. To my daughters, Lydia and Lauren, you both are my pride and joy. There will never be words that I can use to describe how proud I am to call you my girls. To the most important woman in my life, Shanita LaShae Le'Det. I know when you read this you will know the difficulties that came with all that I am today. None of it was possible without you, you are the reason I go hard, and I stay with it because you deserve nothing but the best of me. I am still a work in process, but I will continue to live my purpose and that includes you.

Shirrod Le'Det is a business owner, author, professor, coach, and entrepreneur who challenges the traditions of business growth and leadership development within today's business environments. He has an Executive MBA from Strayer University Jack Welch Management Institute Program, where he graduated with honors. After earning his Executive MBA from the Jack

Welch Management Institution, he attained an adjunct instructor position at Simmons College of Kentucky in Louisville teaching Foundations of Law & Business, Foundations of Management, and Entrepreneurship and Innovation. That position was unique, as it gave him the opportunity to go from learning to teach, and also inspired his love of coaching. When he started working with college students, emerging leaders, small business owners, and church leaders, it led him to become a Growth Coach.

"I help business owners, managers, and self-employed professionals gain clarity about who they are, what they want, and where they are going; allowing them to maximize their time and talents to drive their success and balance their lives".

JOHN JAMERSON

THE VOICES THAT LEAD ME

As I reflect and see the person that I am today, a son, brother, friend, father, husband of 37 years, entrepreneur, visionist, engineer, EMT, paralegal, strategist, historian, farmer, and a minister to list a few. I realize that there are so many who have contributed to my life, some purposely, some unknowingly, some for a reason, and some for a season. I am grateful for them all, I aim to not let their work in me be in vain.

I must however give reverence to those who were the foundation and most impactful in my development. I will begin with the grand matriarch in the family, Julietta Webb Clardy, my paternal grandmother, whom I lovingly refer to as Gran. She was the most sophisticated, hardest working, sharpest dressed, and eloquent speaker that I know. Her soft and pleasant voice gave me the wisdom that guides my life today.

Gran's deep roots and family ties to Brandon, Mississippi gave insight into her love for family, hard work ethic, and wisdom. She often spoke of her maternal grandfather Ol 'man John Watts, who owned all of Rankin County and had it taken away due to a heated dispute that led to the death of his best friend.

Gran often warned me of my temper and the importance to deal with issues early to keep from losing control, to learn conflict resolution. She'd say, "You might not get along with everybody, but you should get along with somebody." She let me know I was part of the equation and the solution.

Gran said to work hard while I'm young and able, so when I'm old I wouldn't have to work hard to survive in my retirement years. She spoke about her grandmother, the Old Lady, saving over $200,000 by selling eggs $0.10 a dozen and butter $.05 a pound daily.

Her paternal grandfather Silas Webb bought 160 acres in Brandon, Mississippi, known as the old homestead, 130 acres is still owned by family. Gran's prized possession: she'd say, "This is the land my grandfather gave me, give it to your grandchildren." We would drive in a caravan of cars with all my great aunts, uncles, and kinfolk from Indianapolis to Jackson, Mississippi filled with blankets and enough food to feed an army. We'd stop at certain gas stations and have a picnic in certain rest areas. My mother feared the south and would tape a dime in our shoes, in case we had to run or got separated, we would have enough to make a phone call. We were instructed about Emmett Till and how we should interact with southern whites

Gran told me she was often teased growing up in Mississippi when she shared what her dream house would look like. When she finally bought her dream home in Indianapolis Gran said she had dreamt about it so much that it wasn't a big deal to her. Often, Gran would tell me to dream about what I want in life and that it would come to pass, to be cautious around dream killers, and seek out those who can dream with me. Gran's home was eloquently decorated, with white walls, gold and crystal fixtures, and Victorian furniture with marble tables. Her basement had a full wet bar and pool table.

Gran was well known for her holiday feasts that would make Hallmark envious of the layout of ethnic foods with 10-15 types of cakes, cobblers, and pies. Gran was a legendary cook, and her home would host upwards of 100 people. It was a labor of love, days of preparation, everything made from scratch, everything from the rooter to the tooter, greens cabbage, butterbean, black-eyed peas, peach cobbler, dressing, and mac and cheese to die for. All the family was required to bring something, but it had to be approved and a masterpiece, you never knew which dignitary or celebrity might make an appearance.

People would start in the kitchen where both counters were full of food to the stove, down the stairs to the pool table covered with the best of southern hospitality, in the corner an old cooker full of wrinkles also known as chitlins. Gran gave what my siblings and I would refer to as the Granny helping, when she would fix your plate, she would tell you to say "when" and then give you two more scoops. She would give more than what was asked for, that was her motto, this applied to love and war. This kept people from being overly greedy and let them know when to back up.

Gran included her fashion tips that I passed down to my sons. When looking for a suit, she'd say "choose from a single-breasted, double-breasted, or three-piece suit, because "class is always in style."

Gran passed down her wisdom to all her grandchildren, she lived well into her 90's and to see 4 generations behind her. In the end, although, we wanted her to live forever, she let it be known that it's "not the quantity of life but the quality of life." I remember when I was in my teens, someone asked Gran why she spent so much time with her grandchildren and she replied, "I want to spend time with them while they're young because when they get older, they may not have time for me." I later told Gran that I would always have time for her, and I'm satisfied to say she was surrounded by all her grandchildren, great-grandchildren, and her only child my father at the time of her transition.

The great influence of my life would include my parents. My parents were married as college sweethearts and stayed married for 40 years. My father Thomas Jamerson Sr. (Chief) was an only child and his parents divorced when he was a child. He remembers when his father was getting ready to go off to war, he introduced my father to a wino on the corner and asked the wino to keep an eye on his son while he was gone. One day my father was not paying attention and began to cross the street when suddenly the wino grabbed him and pulled him back just as a car came streaking by. Chief would always pass the lesson he learned that day to my brother TJ and me, to always be respectful to others from the wino to the president because you never know which one would be there to save your life. Chief taught us to never overestimate or underestimate others or ourselves, that we are no better nor any worse than the next man.

Chief taught TJ and me to be entrepreneurs and the philosophy of being your own boss. Our first job at the age of 6 and 7 was delivering newspapers. We learned that we are responsible for the work we did for others, and they were relying on us to deliver, this tied in with the hard work ethic Gran has taught us. We mowed lawns and shoveled snow, whatever it took to make money within boundaries.

My mother, Elizabeth Harmon, was from Washington, Indiana, a small country town, where everyone knew everyone. They had a farm, where TJ and I would spend our summers. I loved the outdoor country life. My mother who we call MD was beautiful, intelligent, and a great cook with a farm girl work ethic.

One of my earliest memories was of MD reading the Bible to TJ and me. I was fascinated by the stories and couldn't wait to hear what happened next.

MD taught TJ and me how to cook, do laundry, sew, and change a diaper (my sister was 6 years younger than I was). One day while baking cookies the aroma of the cocoa was more than TJ and I could bear, and we pleaded with MD to let us have a spoon full of raw cocoa. She tried to warn us that we needed to wait until she had mixed it with the other ingredients, but we pressured her that much more. MD gave us both a spoon and said enjoy. It was the nastiest, most bitter thing I had tasted. MD said sometimes you have to give people what they ask for, it's not your fault if they don't like it. I learned my lesson, but I was always pushing the boundaries. MD said "life is too short to learn everything by experience, some things I would have to take someone's word of advice". The example she gave was "I don't have to get shot by a gun to learn that a bullet can kill me".

MD gave me my passion for black history. Growing up in Washington, Indiana, she was never taught about black history. After her mother and oldest brother passed away in her late teens, she attended Livingston College where she learned about black history and all the great things, we as a people had done. She vowed that her children would always know about their history. This played an important role in my life with the pro-black, civil rights, and power to the people movements in my formative years. It was also what landed my wife in my college years. MD was a great motivator, when things didn't go my way or the way I had hoped, she would find that something to give a glimmer of hope.

I had prepared my whole high school career to become a veterinarian at Purdue University and play football. Chief's wish was for me to become an engineer with my strong math and science skills. I dropped veterinarian school and signed up for engineering school at Purdue in the last quarter of my senior year at Arlington High School. I didn't make it into engineering school due to it being full and I lost my place getting into veterinarian school. Growing up MD went to school with the President of Vincennes University, which didn't have a football team. She drove me down and we met with Dr. Phil Summers. He told me that all of Vincennes engineering credits would be accepted by Purdue University if I wanted to be transferred.

As MD and I left campus she decided to take me on a black history trip to a small town called Lyles Station. On the 30-minute drive south of Vincennes she told me of the many interesting things about Lyles Station and our family ties. She took me past miles of cornfields to Wayman Chapel Church and the schoolhouse. I thought to myself "I'll never see this place again." I ultimately went to engineering school at Vincennes that fall and the following year met the love of my life, Denise Greer. Upon asking Denise where she was from, she shyly said a little place you never heard of called Lyles Station. I said let me tell you about Lyles Station and proceeded to tell her all that I had learned from my mother. I prided myself on remembering every phone number, address, birthday, and anniversary of all friends and family. This played well with a history that I enjoyed learning about. Denise was highly impressed, and this little tidbit of information gave me the advantage needed to win her over.

MD always had that motherly love, spirituality, and wisdom to guide me to be who I am today. When I was at the height of my lowness, doing the things that weren't beneficial, MD was the one who would encourage me to return to church for my family's sake. MD was the sweetener needed to get me to make the correct decisions. Although I understood the consequences of my actions and accepted them, I had to learn to take someone's advice and not learn everything from experience.

My brother was my greatest opponent, best friend, business partner, teammate, and role model. TJ is 16 months older than I, and we were commonly known as Tommy and Johnny to friends and family growing up. We considered ourselves the Dynamic Duo, that together no one can defeat us. This holds true to this day. Highly competitive, seasoned with sibling rivalry, we took no prisoners. TJ viewed himself as the best there was and only to keep the peace, I let him think that. My job, unknown to TJ, was to support his view of himself to all others. If we were comic book characters, TJ was Spiderman, intelligent with great strength and ability. I was his silent partner, the Incredible Hulk, just as intelligent and the harder you pressed us , the harder, we would come. We kept score on everything from chess to cards and one thing no one wanted was to be placed on our "Wall of Lames." TJ was known as Killa T and I was J Ruthless (Later changed to J Roofless to indicate no limit to my upward boundary after having children) to our friends. I bought our childhood home from MD and Chief, it was the place of competition and great conversations of wisdom and debates. Friends and family would come and bond with us, it helped us to sharpen our skills and our mind. TJ made his power moves in the executive arena I was the defender of the oppressed and defenseless.

At my supervisory job, I was approached by management about a discrimination lawsuit some of the people under my supervision filed. The company demoted them on a bias screening that favored white trainees over these tenured black employees. When asked to back the company against their lawsuit I agreed, if they could provide what had happened in the 30 days that followed a performance review that rated them at 93% or higher. As a result, I was targeted and filed a class action discrimination suit against the company, in which I prevailed. During the lawsuit, I studied to become a paralegal, so I could better understand the laws governing me. The lawsuit lasted 5 years, the company told me that they would hold it up to 10 years before we would make it to court. I politely told them that they were on notice that in 10 years I would still be there standing firm. The disheartening part is that I lost my supervisory position and was demoted to a starting position while keeping my pay. I often wanted to quit, during the case, but I could hear MD saying, "wrong is wrong, even when everyone is doing it and right is right, even when no one is doing it." I give all credit to The Most High, for the victory. There were executives in the corporate office that decided to close two facilities that were under the jurisdiction of my lawsuit, costing over 2,000 people their jobs, many were my friends. I went into a deep depression, believing my actions harmed those I was hoping to help. It was years later while teaching my son how to ride his bicycle in front of my house, that a former co-worker driving down the street slammed on his brakes and jumped out of the car. He said he had been looking for me to thank me, he was never promoted at the company where we worked, but since they closed, he made it to an executive position in Chicago. He said this would have never happened if he stayed at that job. My heart was lifted, as I realized what Pastor J.A. Johnson said that 'we are to do what God has directed us to do, it is God's job to get His desired results.'

Now both my sons have businesses, one is a barber like my grandfather and the other a farmer like my father-in-law. I'm advocating on behalf of my people, the oppressed and underserved. The black farmers and urban food deserts (food apartheid) are at the forefront of my efforts. Legacy Taste of the

Garden and Legacy Farming and Health group are both businesses that I direct. I'm following in the footsteps of my forefathers and standing on their shoulders. We all have a legacy from the past and we are the creators of the legacy for our children. We should act wisely in the actions we take, considering that everything we do has an influence on ourselves and others, and strive for the positive effect.

My influencers were like ingredients for baking a cake from scratch, some good, some sweet, some bitter, and some that help to blend it. Some add heat, some are the icing, and others are the nuts. All of them have influenced me to be what I am today, doing my best to serve YAH (God), Family, and country. A shout out to my wife Denise, who loves me with all my flaws, my sons DeAnthony and Jayson, who are the reason I face all my fears so they can go twice as far in half the time, Cousin Pam Webb, who makes sure I keep my passport ready, Aunt Carolyn who taught me to utilize all my resources. Cousin Ron Lacey, Rev. Dre Benson, Kelvin Jarret, Marky Mark, Baba Kamau, Dr. Boyce Watkins, RCA Elders, Arlington class of 82, and Vincennes University family. We are the iron that sharpens iron, all I do is with us all in mind. Special shout out to A.M. Noel and Stan Matthews who made this all possible.

John Jamerson is the Project Director of the family-owned farm Legacy Taste of the Garden. John provides technical and strategic experience in creating the visionary outline, collaborating with individuals and organizations to create a sustainable business in agriculture. John's responsibilities include building a sustainable farm structure, marketing, and training modules in agriculture for socially disadvantaged farmers, youths and communities, managing partnerships, programs, developing markets to provide fresh produce to the community and working with different organizations and stores.

VIOLETTEE V. BROWN

AND STILL, WE RISE

IRENE PRESSLEY BROWN

*"Do not pray for an easy life; pray for the strength to endure
a difficult one."*
Bruce Lee

My mother, Irene Deloris Pressley Brown, was born in 1932 during the Great Depression. She was also born Black in the State of South Carolina. Some would say the deck was stacked against her, but God is good. My grandparents were able to provide enough of the essentials to make a decent life for their 10 children during some lean years.

She attended Zion Elementary and High Schools, two Rosenwald educational institutions for students of color in Orangeburg County. She often thought that teaching would be a desirable profession. Many of her teachers were educated women of color and role models in the community. However, she also knew that she didn't have money for college – after all, she had nine other siblings in her family.

During her senior year of high school, the Roper School of Nursing in Charleston opened its doors to students of color. As Judge Constance Baker Motley often said, *"Something which we think is impossible now is possible in another decade."* Recognizing the need for more medically trained professionals in her community, my mother applied and was accepted to Roper's practical nursing program. She graduated in 1953 and went to work for Orangeburg Regional Hospital, now the Regional Medical Center (RMC).

Around the same time, she would marry her high school sweetheart and they would begin rearing a family that would grow to four children. Three years into their marriage, she and my father would purchase 30 acres of land that included a small house and farmland. Her nursing credentials would pay off during these early years because it allowed my mother to earn a steady paycheck while my father worked to make the farm profitable. She worked at RMC for 43 years.

Rearing a family was challenging, however, doing so in the 1960s would prove even more difficult as my mother and father along with others in the community got involved in civil rights protests and local boycotts of racist business practices in South Carolina. I was too young to understand much of what was happening around me, but my mother's eyes told a different story. A story of being sick and tired of Jim Crow laws and a way of life that she did not want for her children. She would always say, *"We must put our trust in the good Lord. He will see us through this."*

Working as a nurse at RMC had its benefits, but it also had its challenges. My mother did not live an easy life, but through her faith in God Almighty and the foundation laid by her ancestors, she was able to endure some challenging circumstances. She often encountered difficult co-workers and patients who wanted to work with someone other than herself. Needless to say, she figured out a way to manage *"dem folks"*. Accolades over the years would come from patients and staff. She was often presented with gifts from patients in appreciation for her caregiving role and the many things she said or did to make their stay at RMC tolerable.

My mother was a Christian woman and a praying woman. I would often find her on her knees after a long difficult night at work. She instilled in me and my siblings the importance of prayer and the need to spend some quiet time with God. She didn't pray for an easy life, but the strength to endure what came her way. As life would have it, her faith was tested. At the age of 39 she developed pneumonia, a heart condition, and other maladies that compromised her immune system. She was only given six months to live. She prayed that God would spare her life to see her children reach adulthood. He did. She never stopped trusting God.

She loved singing and listening to gospel music. She became a Christian at an early age and served in many leadership positions within the Macedonia Baptist Church including President of the Gospel Choir and mid-week worship service leader. She was also secretary of the Orangeburg-Orthodox Baptist Sunday School Convention and a board member of the Bull Swamp Live Working Ushers & Choirs Convention.

My mother was also a major initiator and contributor to the ongoing success of the Pressley Family Reunions which began in 1985. She departed this earthly life on November 19, 2006. Although she has been gone for 15+ years, her light is still shining today within me, my family members, and so many others whose lives she touched in her brief stay on this earth.

LEROY B. BROWN, SR. M.D.

"You have been assigned this mountain to show others it can be moved." Mel Robbins

My paternal uncle, Leroy Bradford Brown, Sr., was born on June 5, 1929, in Detroit, MI. Shortly afterwards, his father died of meningitis forcing his mother, Fannie, to return to South Carolina with two young children. They moved in with her father, Charlie Hubbard, locally known as *Boss Charlie* to most people. Boss Charlie was blessed to own a 426-acre farm. It took significant labor to operate a farm of this size. At one time or another, Boss Charlie employed most of his children in his farming operations.

Leroy was convinced that only an education would save him from a life spent plowing and viewing the backside of a mule. Intelligent and hardworking, he completed high school by age 15 with the hopes of going to college. However, after a *falling out* with Boss Charlie over the wages that he was not being paid, he went to live and work with his Uncle Ebbie

Hubbard who trained him to be a master carpenter – a skill he would use for the rest of his life.

At 17, he joined the United States Marine Corp (USMC) because a recruiter told him that *coloreds* were allowed to fly fighter planes. Of course, this turned out to not be true. While in the Corp, he hoped to be selected for an overseas assignment and see another part of the world. His commanding officer valued his typing skills more than his quest for bravado. He stayed at Camp LeJeune and was honorably discharged as a corporal in 1952.

Although he couldn't fly the planes he loved, he did pursue the greatest love of his life, for it was in the Marines that he first glimpsed the photo of a young woman named Ola Augusta Watkins. He begged his good friend and her brother, Price Watkins, for her address and promptly began writing to her. He proposed three times before she agreed to marry him. The third time she let it be known that she wanted to marry a doctor. Leroy, who had been hoping to become an aeronautical engineer, quickly let her know that it was his lifelong dream to become a doctor. When she finally said "Yes", he took no chances and whisked her across the state line to Arkansas where they were married on the same day - January 3, 1952.

Leroy went to college on the GI Bill and graduated from South Carolina State College with all *A's* except for a *C* in French. He was accepted to the University of South Carolina School, School of Medicine, a *whites only* school at that time. The state would pay his tuition if he attended the local *colored* medical school. Leroy raised the stakes: He would take the state's tuition offer only if he could attend Howard University's medical school in Washington, DC.

Leroy earned his medical degree with a specialty in internal medicine from Howard in 1958. Following his residency at Fresno County Hospital, he and his family moved to Sacramento. Together, Leroy and Ola opened a private practice in internal medicine. Ola was the nurse, receptionist, typist, etc. Leroy would also work for the Department of Corrections treating prison inmates later in his career.

He also achieved his dream and life-long ambition of learning to fly an airplane and earning his pilot's license. His pilot's license and later private pilot instrument rating opened up Act II of his professional career. These new credentials helped him secure an assignment with the Federal Aviation Administration (FAA) as a medical examiner. He was able to share his love of aviation and God with a number of pilots, some who became life-long friends.

My uncle especially enjoyed sharing his love for God with others. He and his wife were members of the Church of God Seventh Day Adventist. They were also children of the Great Depression. Each experienced their share of tough times; however, they were not afraid of hard work. They also wanted better opportunities for their children and others. From humble beginnings, my uncle moved mountains in his lifetime.

My uncle and his wife played a pivotal role in assisting me in shaping my adult life and professional career when I was a student at Howard University. They generously poured their knowledge and wisdom into me and treated me like I was one of their children. I often referred to them as my *west coast mom and dad.* I was fortunate to have the opportunity to visit with them often. Sad and tragically, our family would lose two incredibly gifted and generous people on June 2, 2016 when they succumbed to injuries from a vehicle accident that occurred a week earlier. They are sorely missed.

JAMES B. MAVIS

"Conflict is inevitable, but combat is optional." **Max Lucado**

I've had the opportunity to work with some well-respected individuals during my time in corporate America and in my own business. During three short years with my first employer, Procter & Gamble (P&G), I gained skills as a process/product engineer with significant engineering design and construction experience. The training and mentoring that was provided set the stage for my future work with other employers and my own business. I am also happy to share with you that I was a part of the P&G team that introduced Buttered Flavored Crisco.

I was wooed away from P&G by my second employer, CH2M Hill – an international consulting firm. In additional to my technical expertise, they valued the hands-on and field experience that accompanied my knowledge of process/product design – something that most engineers in this new company did not have. About a year-and-a-half into this assignment, I encountered two supervisors who I often referred to as the evil twins. Each decided that I wasn't a good fit in the organization because *they said so*.

Not fitting in is one thing, but accusing a person of being incompetent is another. When that didn't work, my writing skills were attacked. I was cleared of these accusations, but knew more would come. If I didn't have enough problems, a situation arose on a major project with a subcontractor that required intervention by senior leaders. James "Jim" Mavis, the Principal Technologist for chemical processes, was called in to meet with the team in my office. It was agreed that I along with the male evil twin who I will call "Roger" would work with Jim to develop a new project strategy. Already feeling deflated by the earlier struggles, I thought to myself: *I'm toast! He will probably also think that I am incompetent, and I will get fired!*

Feeling reluctant, I started to piece together my part of the assignment. My work needed to be completed a week later for the next face-to-face meeting. After some research and data analysis, I began building a spreadsheet of my findings. Three days later, I made a conscientious decision to touch bases with Jim to ensure that I was on track in my approach and to minimize any wrong turns. He suggested that I send him a copy. He would review it on the plane ride to our next meeting. I did that.

The next day, *Roger* stopped by my office to inquire about my progress on the assignment. I was working on the assignment at that time plugging data into the spreadsheet. After sharing some of my findings with him, he asked me if I would print him a copy so that he could get a better look at the numbers. Seeing no harm in his request, I did that.

We are now at Friday and the second team meeting. After some status updates about the project and the contract, Jim turned to me and my coworker and said, "Why don't you two update us on the work that you've done." Before I could speak, Roger opens a folder and says, "Here Jim, I want you to take a look at this spreadsheet I've been working on." I could see that this was my spreadsheet that he was passing to the Principal Technology Officer. After someone calls you incompetent, you don't expect them to take credit for your work! There are few times that I have been speechless! This was one of those times!

Jim took a look at the spreadsheet, he looked at me, and then he looked at *Roger*. He looked at me again, and said, *"Roger, Vi and I have already discussed the information in this spreadsheet and this looks very much like the copy that I reviewed this morning."* In telling this story, I am sharing the beginning of my relationship with Jim Mavis who was highly regarded within CH2M Hill and his peers within industry.

What Jim did that day is not something that everyone would do. One of the key attributes of a mentor is that he or she has your back. My chance meeting and opportunity to work with him was the beginning of a professional relationship and wonderful friendship that has lasted to this day. Having a mentor at work or other places is important for career success. It is my belief that we would have more women and persons of color in science, technology, engineering, and math (STEM) fields if they had mentors.

I would go on to work with Jim on other assignments. Not only did he have my back in the workplace, but he also shared his knowledge of critical thinking and a unique approach to problem solving that has served me well to this day. He is an intellectual lodestar who successfully developed a secret sauce for mentoring and training. By his actions, he also proved to me that conflict is inevitable, but combat is optional.

Growing up in a southern rural community during the 1960s was a period that not only shaped me, but this country. My humble beginnings in Orangeburg, SC laid a foundation for the fortitude that my future would require. Three key individuals who I consider to be *earthly potters* are highlighted in the preceding pages. Some of the folks who also poured into me their love, knowledge and wisdom are spotlighted here.

I am very thankful to family and friends who showed an interest in my education as I matriculated from elementary school to college. At Howard University, I would gain a new family of friends that included faculty members, staff, and fellow alumni. Howard University has proven to be one of the best decisions and experiences of my life.

My first two employers, P&G and CH2M Hill, provided a solid foundation for technical and leadership skills. Thank you to Mark Jarvis and Bill Hagen for their assistance in my engineering training at P&G, and to Mike DeFillipo and Dr. Jill Shapiro for believing in me and my abilities at CH2M Hill. The fundamental skills learned in both organizations have been applied over and over again.

Credit is also given to faculty and staff of Arizona State University's Executive MBA program for their assistance when I became unemployed in the middle of my studies. Thank you to Rose Presley-Alston for respite care and new experiences, and to the members of the Matthews Business Network for a new direction in business and life.

Last but not least, I acknowledge my spiritual adviser, Dr. Warren H. Stewart, Sr., of First Institutional Baptist Church (Phoenix, AZ). He is a master teacher whose preaching and prayers have fed my soul. *If it had not been for the Lord on my side, where would I be?*

Violettee V. Brown *is CEO and Founder of Vi Brown Speaks and Prophecy Consulting Group. She wears several baseball caps including strategist, thought leader, inspirational and motivational speaker, business & STEM consultant, blogger, and book reviewer. As a professional speaker, Vi believes that one's understanding of STEM and other topics can be enhanced at any age. Why? Because doing so creates opportunities for everyone – uplifting communities, improving access for others and sustaining our planet. She also offers solutions for how to do this.*

Brown is also the recipient of numerous awards and honors including Past President of the Society of Women Engineers and Guest Ambassador and Tour Leader - Women in Engineering Delegation Tour of China. Vi holds a BS and MS in chemical engineering from Howard University and an MBA from Arizona State University. Connect with her at www.vibrownspeaks.com and vibrownspeaks@gmail.com. Visit my blog, A Bridge for Business & STEM, and connect with me on LinkedIn.

RODNEY C. BURRIS

LIVING IN 3D

DEXTER L. BINDER:

When I was about 12 years old, there was a gentleman in my life who used to give me free haircuts. Now I know that may not sound like a big deal, but for me at the time it meant the world.

You see I was dealing with the brand new realization that we were poor. -- Actually this wasn't a *brand new* realization; it just was the latest iteration of it. You see there have been times in my life when we didn't have much food in the house for long stretches of time. There's also been times when the total amount of clothes that I had was so few in number that with my best ability to space them out I was wearing the same outfit every Monday, the same outfit every Tuesday, etc. -- This was one of the hardest times in my life and I never would have imagined that this would've been my reality, yet I found myself there.

So fast forward to when I met Dex. He owned a barbershop that was a long way away from my house and somehow it seemed to my mother and I that it was the closest one to us. I lived with her and two younger sisters then. My mom didn't have a lot of money and life was always about scraping up enough to make ends meet, and not having enough to do any splurging or extravagance at all. We lived a life of bare necessities only. -- And one of the things that was considered a luxury was regular haircuts for me. So needless to say those were sacrificed, often going long stretches (weeks...months) without a haircut. I didn't have a high *sense of self* back then (although it did always seem like people liked my presence & company).

It was one of the most challenging, sinking, suffocating periods of my life. I didn't feel seen, heard nor valued. So by the time Dex offered me my first haircut, the moment was magical.

It was early on a random Saturday morning, and we were on our way to church. I grew up in a church that held services on Saturdays. And my mother was an influential person in the church, so she needed to be there for every major event, especially the Saturday services. Because of this, it was always a struggle to try to convince mom to part with her few dollars and take me way up the street to the barbershop, wait around until it was complete, then take me back home so that we can wash and prepare for church.

On this fateful day, I had endured a particularly rough dosage of good ol' moms straight talk on the reality of our situation: the need for thrift & budgeting, the virtue in acknowledging that although uncomfortable our lot in life was not for us to spend lavishly on things like haircuts, especially when the location was so far out of the way with a tight schedule to uphold. She wasn't being mean, she just simply needed her oldest child to understand the realities of our situation.

Always proud of my independence, which I displayed from a very young age, she and I made an agreement that I could go on that particular morning *if* I were comfortable riding my bike those several miles back to our home. I agreed because I knew that my mom was carrying a lot and taking a risk, yet she wanted to please me for being a good son.

When I walked into the shop that day, Dex saw my face and immediately asked me what was wrong. I explained to him our situation (which he already was somewhat aware of). And out of the kindness of his heart, he not only offered to throw my bike in the back of his vehicle and give me a ride home, he also made a deal with me that as long as my grades were good, he would give me a free haircut. -- That one simple gesture (well, two) gave me new life!

All of a sudden, I had a reason to do well in school. I had a reason to hold my head up high, knowing that a newly fresh cut was just around the corner. My mom had given me permission to get there, if I was willing to make the ride, and Dex was willing to reward me for being a good student.

Dexter L Binder positively changed my life for the better, simply by sharing with me his time, his craft, and giving me his validation. It is my honor to openly and humbly say,

"Dex, YOU Influenced Me!"

DARNELL SMITH

It was a random Friday afternoon. I was walking with a group of boys, all of whom were between the ages of 12-14. I was right there smack-dab in the middle of them (both in age (13) and in physical placement (walking in the center of the group)). At the time, we lived in an apartment complex, and me and my crew spent a lot of time around each other playing basketball, playing Sega/super Nintendo, and listening to music. We felt like we were the up and coming crew; or to use bball vernacular, *we had next.*

You see there was another group of boys, several years older than us. They were between 17 to 19 and we thought they were simply the coolest guys out anywhere. Period. They played basketball too, but they rarely let us play with them because we were too little to run with them. They seemed to have all the older girls that we wanted, always had a little bit of money, and always seemed like they were just *chillaxin.* We wanted to be just like them (I know I did).

On this random Friday afternoon, as I was walking in the middle of my own crew, one of those older guys came up behind us. He said he needed some help; that he had a shipment coming in and wanted us to help move it. "You get half of whatever you sell, you sell 50 you get 25, you sell 100 you get 50."

Now what you don't know is that this conversation happened at a time when once again my family didn't have a lot of money. My dad was gone, my mother was struggling both emotionally and financially, and my sisters needed shoes and food and a little more than the bare basic necessities.

So listening to him, I slowed down while my crew kept

walking. I moved from the middle…to the back (both literally and figuratively; because although my boys heard the same conversation I was hearing, I seemed to be the only one that was listening. The other boys seemed disinterested, almost as if he didn't say those dollar amounts; almost as if they weren't just financially struggling as we were in my family; almost as if we all wouldn't have just jumped at the chance to hang with those big older dudes).

Yet, there I was, in the back of the pack both in thought and pole-positioning, although deep down I knew that what I was considering was wrong and would ultimately become one of the worst decisions of my life. I still was very much intrigued. -- In fact, I was more than intrigued. I was *Down*. All it took was just one more of my boys, or *shute* anything, and I would have totally went with ol buddy.

Around this time in my life, there was a popular new song that had just come out by the now legendary artist, Tupac Amaru Shakur. The song was entitled "Dear Mama", and it outlined the struggles he had growing up with a single mother who was doing the best she could to raise him and his sister. He rapped about not understanding her decisions and directions back then, and how he gave her a hard time too, with some of his rebellious antics.

Most poignantly for me back then, he rhymed: *"I hung around with the thugs, and even though they sold drugs they showed a young brother love."* His lyrics go on to say, *"I moved out, started really hanging I need a money on my own so I started slanging* [i.e., selling drugs], *I ain't guilty cause even though I sell rocks, it feels good putting money in your mailbox."*

This was very much how I felt. It was tough to see my mother struggling and I wanted to help. I also just wanted more food in the house. But most importantly, I think I was just looking for a way out.

Miraculously, Mr. Darnell Smith entered the picture. -- Mr. D (as I like to call him) was like a mentor to me who took me under his wing a short while before this fateful afternoon. He had a son that was a little bit younger than I was, and would often pick me up and take us to go eat or to the movies or just hang out.

Well on this particular day Mr. D decided to leave work early and come get me for an impromptu *burger and fries* with him and his kid, Lil D. -- The same day that I was lingering behind listening to the older boy talk to us about the profits of selling drugs.

It seems it some moment of divine clarity, providence and inspiration, Mr. D listened to his higher calling, left work in enough time to pull up next to me before the conversation got too far out of hand. That miraculous intervention reset my life's course and re-righted my ship. I stay in touch with Mr. D until this day; he influenced me.

Darryl Glen McCoy

"Don't be so heavenly minded, Chris,
that you are no earthly good..."

These were the words I heard over the hum of the clippers as I sat in a kitchen getting my haircut. I was perhaps about 15 years old, and I was nearing the tail end of one of the worst periods of my life. I was so miserable, so unhappy. I felt so unloved, so un-valued, so unseen -- So unreachable. Although I didn't have the words to express it at the time, the reality was that I was merely existing but I wasn't really alive. I was a shell of myself closed off within myself.

Three years prior to then, my Dad had left us for the final time. I went through a series of fights, suspensions, and school transitions (three within 3 years). I didn't know myself, who I was, what I wanted, nor what I needed. So I conformed to survive in the new school environments. Sometimes I was a bad ass kid. Sometimes I was a super smart honor roll student. Sometimes I was the proper and respectful young man, and yet sometimes I didn't care at all about my grades. Whatever it was I needed to be, I just wanted to do that so I could get along; even if that meant selling myself out. I didn't like the me that

I had become, and I was tired of it. But I didn't know just how ready for a Change (any change) I was.

One summer night, my church was hosting an outdoor service under very large (expansive) carnival-esque tents. We held services a lot back in those days, both indoors and outdoors, at least 4 times a week, every single week. Being as my mom was one of the administrators of the church, we were present for every... single... service... For years.

I share that simply to point out that there was nothing particularly special about the invocations happening that night. I had heard them all before. But this time, there was a major difference. -- I MYSELF was different. I had wanted to halt the falling, the screeching, the emotional shapeshifting. So in a moment of boldness that turned to be one of the most ground-shaking Kairos moments of my life, I stood up in church raised my hands, and stated that I was ready to fully give myself over to GOD, at all costs, no matter what, regardless of what that looked like.

I meant those words, and I was ready to commit. It wasn't long before I found myself digging deeper and deeper into God, into the church...and into religiosity. I penned lyrics years later commemorating this period of my life:

> *In a flash son, the boy was older, getting bolder -- he was a man, son.*
> *But really he wasn't, he was weak yet so deter-mined.*
> *Without no figure, still a ******, ain't no wo-man.*
> *He wasn't hard, so at first he tried to trust his God.*
> *Jumped in deep, with both feet,*
> *Man went overboard.*
> *His zeal was heavy so he stayed drowning for bout a year.*
> *Father-figure pulled him up, wisdom into his ear.*

That *father figure* was Darryl Glen McCoy. Darryl Glen McCoy is the founder and overseer of a respectable faith-based conglomerate. His ministry owns several churches that he established all over the United States and has had a presence around other parts of the world. Formally, he was our leader *in the body of Christ.* Informally however, especially for some of the younger folks my age who didn't have a stable dad, we affectionately picked up the nick name, "Pops" for him. It was a name he never requested, but never rejected from us neither. Although he was so busy, I got to spend good quantities of quality-time with him. Fortunately for me he was a little bit more than just the generic *pops* that he was to the masses. His kids went to the same school as I did so I first began to see him most, after school. Sometimes it was convenient for a few of us to carpool. Eventually those turned into weekend hang-outs, etc. Because of this, I got to see him a lot more than just church services. And he began to treat me like a *bonus* son.

This turned out to be one of the most formative relation-ships of my life. I have had the opportunity to accompany him when he was closing major deals, and tag along with him when he was just making minor purchases. I got to see how he han-dled himself in different situations as a Dad, as a businessman, and as a Leader. I got to see him handle conflict with grace, poise and wisdom, and also got to watch him get justifiably angry about situations and choose to metabolize those feelings into productive, restorative actions.

Because I wanted to be like him in so many ways, I found myself living an overly pious, disconnected, and unrealistic life. Yes, I wanted to please God, first & foremost. -- But if I'm being honest, I also wanted to be as pleasing as possible to the only consistent father-type figure in my life at the time. (And even he was inconsistently present, spending most of his time on the road and in airplanes, visiting his churches and checking on his people.)

I believed (based on what I read and what I thought I was learning from church) that a life of pure sacrifice, ostracism and discomfort *for righteousness sake* was the most pleasing thing to God. I was amazingly very good at this type of aus-tere dedication, and it was costing me my emotional health, my relationship health (sisters, mom, friends) and also my literal physical health (due to all the fasting). I was miserable. And I lived under the constant mental pressure that I although I was going to heaven, I still wasn't *good enough* yet in God's eyes for the greater rewards. Thus, I was nowhere near done with tragedy; in fact it probably was gonna get worse as I increased my capability to ignore my own well-being in pursuit of a perceived greater good.

So in the midst of my despair, and at the height of my loneliness and in the throes of my self-imposed exile...Pops spoke one of the most groundbreaking phrases I ever heard. As he held the clippers to my head to give me a fresh new blend, he said, *"Chris, you cannot be so heavenly minded that you are no earthly good."*

WOW. Never had I thought before that I needed to be good for anybody nor anything, in this world. I thought that everything in this world was bad, and was the result of a preternatural falling from grace. I assumed that the ultimate show of spiritual readiness and growth was to be as aloof, as unphased and as disconnected from Earth as possible -- that the real rewards was in heaven after we die, and that until then we are to *suffer like good little soldiers* to gain even greater rewards later. -- In that one simple phrase, the man that I respected the most at that time of my life told me that there was such a thing as balance even in this Christian Walk, and that I should recalibrate my current approach. It was paradigm-shifting, and it pulled me up out of despair and help me re-right the ship.

I could go on and on about the many ways pops has positively impacted me in irreversible ways. I'll some it up here by simply saying,

Darryl Glen McCoy, YOU influenced Me.

Rodney C Burris is one of the nation's top leaders in unlocking human potential and inspiring organizations to greatness. Raised in the inner cities of Baltimore and Jacksonville,

Rodney is the son of a hardworking single mother. Because his father often battled substance abuse, the family spent time in a homeless shelter and endured poverty and domestic abuse. Despite this adversity, Rodney still earned a bachelor's degree in Psychology from The Johns Hopkins University and a master's in Nonprofit Management from Capella University.

Rodney has assisted numerous companies with team-building, communication, data evaluation and program development. His workshops and seminars are among the most popular in the United States and abroad.

"LET ME HELP YOUR TEAM OVER ACHIEVE!"

SHANESE CARR

YOU ARE YOUR BROTHER'S KEEPER

Josephine Campbell of Fayetteville, NC known to me by way of Granny and known to her community as "Mama Joe" was all about praising God, learning lessons from and appreciating nature and serving others as a way of life.

Before starting school I spent most of the week with my grandmother in church or at a church function. Granny was a part of the church choir and they were legendary. We would travel from church to church and my Granny would have on the most beautiful dresses and hats and sing with so much joy to the heavens above. I remember one day I was highly upset because I wanted to stay outside and play and Granny called me inside the house, had me take a bath and she looked at me with her beautiful chocolate face and smile over her glasses while I was in the tub when I asked her "Granny why do we have to go to church so much?"

Granny pushed her glasses back up on her nose as she looked up to the ceiling closed her eyes took a breath in and let it out slow then opened her eyes looked back down at my wondering and waiting eyes. She touched my face and said "Nese, There is a power bigger than us that watches over us that we cannot see every day. He gave each one of us a special song that the Angels cannot even sing. He gives us breath every day and made the world for us to enjoy! When we sing to him we are praising him and showing him thanks and appreciation for creating us and the world around us to enjoy!" If we don't praise him the rocks will praise him and I don't know about you but I don't want a rock getting the blessings that God has for me!" She touched my nose and had a smile on her face. In that moment I noticed the joy that my Granny spoke with, the light and glint in her eye that she had when she had just spoken this important knowledge to me. So my curious mind asked her "Granny why are you so happy when you talk about God?" She replied, "Needy Beep because I know that God loves me and you no matter what and I am happy to share that love with you there is a power within you that you cannot see!" She then went on to teach me a song called "God Gave Me A Song". I repeated after her happily singing to the top of my lungs in the bathroom soaking in the warm tub, "God gave me a song, that the Angels cannot sing. I've been washed in the blood of the Holy One, I've been redeemed. Sometimes when I am feeling low, no one to care, no place to go, My father is rich in houses and land he holds the power of the world in his hands! Power!!" Not fully understanding the lesson of these words and my grandmother's joy until years to come the seed was yet still planted.

When we were not in church granny had me outside in the yard in her garden. She had one small garden beside her bedroom window downstairs on the left side of the house and another across the yard that was a lot longer near a beautiful hedge. Granny had all types of things growing in her garden. Tomatoes, beans, peas among many others. One day we went outside and Granny had me help her pick these long green things up and put them into a bucket while she was on the other side near her bedroom window taking pretty red plump juicy tomatoes off the vine. We went inside the house downstairs and she showed me how to shell peas and tell the good ones from the bad ones. After we finished we then went upstairs and I sat at the table as I watched Granny put on her apron and wash the vegetables off in the sink. She began cutting the tomatoes into slices and put them on a plate and put a little salt and pepper on the plate and then placed the plate in front of me. After saying grace I ate the tomatoes for the first time and had an explosion of flavor happening in my mouth, I hurriedly and happily ate the rest of the juicy tomatoes with the seasoning and after finishing asked my grandmother while she was preparing the peas to go with dinner, about gardening and how this came from dirt. Granny explained to me that we must appreciate the earth because God made the earth for us to enjoy. We get great results because she showed love and care to the seeds and to the earth, this is why she spoke to her plants. She advised that the dirt and earth nourishes the seeds and we are able to get back what we give. We plant the seeds, nurture them and show them love and God does the rest. She explained that because we showed the seeds love and nurtured them, now their fruit will in turn nurture us. She then explained how everything is an exchange of energy and that eventually everything goes back into the earth including us. She taught me about how the trees help us breathe and we help them breathe and why they are so important to us. She taught me how to look for lessons in the cycles of plants and animals and beings that are around us and learn lesson from nature. That there is a physical meaning to everything as well as a spiritual one beyond what the eye can see. We all serve a purpose and we are here to serve.

In addition to the lesson above Granny was always somewhere helping someone somehow. She would remind me of the lessons that she taught me about how nature serves a purpose to help us and in turn we must serve as well. To this day I still don't know who this man Mr. Trellis is to my Granny. Mr. Trellis was an older man that needed help with a wheelchair because something had happened to his legs and he always had a blue baseball cap on his head that said veteran on the back. We would go to his house every other week and she would clean his house and then bring him back every other Sunday and he would eat dinner with us at my Granny's house. Granny said that she took care of him because he needed help and she cleaned for him because he needed it and if she were in his shoes she would want someone to help her. She then taught me the lesson of serving and treating others as we would like to be treated. She taught me that this was a golden rule and our duty is to serve as nature serves us. We must also serve others.

You are your brother's keeper!

***

Teresa Carr represented the Essence of Elegance so much, that is was the name of her business. I learned that my mother was a force to be reckoned with. She was an Advocate for Black Excellence, Education, and Humanitarianism.

"You so black, if you come to school at night you will be counted absent!" "You so black, when you go outside the sun and the moon fight over the time they are supposed to be out, stay in the classroom so we can have recess in the sun."

I thought I was cute, my mother had pressed my hair and put colorful bows all over in my hair neatly and made me wear a dress to school. She gleamed at me that morning and kissed me on the forehead and told me to have a great day at school. I was in a new city at a new school with people I didn't know. I heard the remarks above all day about my skin color and did not understand why people were being so mean to me about my dark skin. I held my composure and when I got home I boo hoo cried! My mother came in my room when she got in from work and asked me about my day at school. I told her through tears, the horror I had experienced and asked her if we could pray for God to lighten my skin together.

My mother looked at me with a smile and told me that we would not pray for God to lighten my skin but that we would pray for those people because "they know not what they do." She said God uniquely created every inch of my body in detail and that if everyone looked the same the world would be boring. I learned that day that I am special and the culture that I belong to has a rainbow of colors and many before me prayed and sacrificed for me before I was even born so that I may enjoy life. I went to bed after saying my prayers curious that night.

The next morning my alarm went off and I got up and got ready for school, I could hear the song *Gypsy Woman* playing coming from my mother's room as she got ready for work. She came into my room singing "lada dee lada dow" and she told me that I was taking the day off of school to do a field trip to her office. When we got to her office she sat me down in a chair and had me read a book that said *Raleigh-Durham Black Pages*. It was a magazine that showcased local Black Business owners along with resources and events to help strengthen the Black

Community. She explained to me that she was a marketing consultant for the Raleigh-Durham Black pages and her job was to seek out Black Excellence and share them with the world. I kept turning the pages in the book and was shocked when I looked on the page and saw my mother peering up at me from the page with her grey blazer on and royal blue shirt with an article to match. My mother is Black Excellence. At this moment I was filled with joy and proud to see my mother in an article. She said "Nese I don't want you to be like me, I want you to be better than me!" At that moment I knew that I had some huge shoes to fill and tasks in front of me. Later that year my mother gave me a board game for Christmas called Black Americans of Achievement. I learned so much about Black History. I was completely amazed to learn all that my culture had done and that some of the people in my game were still alive!

I then had a new sense of purpose about myself and loved who I was until I went to school in middle school and saw our history book that only had a couple of pages about us in the book. I was upset. I asked my teacher why there were only a couple of pages in the history book about my culture. She told me it was because my people were slaves and people owned us, beat us and worked us. She said "you weren't supposed to know how to read or write, you would be killed for that years ago". I don't remember what obscene response I had to this teacher but I do remember feeling embarrassed and ashamed and so angry that I felt hot. Why would this teacher say this to me with that horrible look on her face? Whatever I said warranted a call from my teacher to my mother. When I got home, I explained what happened to my mother. My mother gave me a reader's digest that day and told me to write the words in the vocabulary section 3 times each, and use them in a sentence. She then advised me to write an essay on respect and give it to the teacher that I apparently disrespected. I had to write what respect was, how it was earned and how it can be shown and why it should be shown to everyone regardless of race, sex or religious background.

After my mother read the paper and approved it, I gave the paper to my teacher and later that day after she read my paper she pulled me to the side and apologized to me for disrespecting me and said that she appreciated me writing that paper for her. When I got home I told my mother and she told me it was good that my teacher apologized and then she went on to teach me about slavery and the Civil Rights Movement, including sacrifices and what those before me had done to ensure that I had an equal chance at life. She taught me that knowledge is power and to appreciate their sacrifices. From that day on, every week I had to write the vocabulary words from the reader's digest and memorize and recite verses from the Bible to her. She told me "listen sweetheart, someone can take your house, your clothes, your car, anything you have materialistic but they cannot take who you are and what you know! You make it a point to learn something new every day and keep a student mentality, you can survive anything with knowledge."

Teresa Carr wasn't about educating me. She wanted to ensure that other children were educated as well. Remember when I said my mother exuded the Essence of Elegance so much that it was her business name? My mother had a modeling agency by the name of Essence of Elegance, Inc. She would organize, promote, and host fashion shows to benefit the United Negro College Fund, The National Black Child Development Institute and Interact as a way of giving back or paying it forward into the community. I remember we were at T-Bone Junction Steakhouse off Six Forks Road in Raleigh, NC and Gayle Hurd, Jim Payne, Dwayne Ballen, Cy Young and Donna Gregory were all seated at the table with my mother and I. I was so nervous to be sitting at the table with all these people that I either saw on TV or heard on the radio. When I tell you I was going back and forth to the bathroom every ten minutes, I am serious.

Donna Gregory came in the bathroom and used it. She came beside me while I was at the sink washing my hands. My eyes were so big I felt they were going to pop out of my head and I was just staring in shock. She said "Sweetie, why are you so nervous?" I replied stammering "because you are all on TV you are famous!" She turned and looked at me after drying her hands and throwing her paper towel in the garbage and said "Listen, I am just like you love, I laugh, cry, get angry, get nervous and all we are no different. I just sit in front of a camera and share what's going on in the world but I am just another human being just like you. If you ever need me for anything I am here". She gave me a hug and proceeded out the bathroom and, in that moment, I looked in the mirror and said ,"wow my mom knows some really awesome people"! When I finished in the bathroom and went back to the table, my mother had her Best Friend Donald E Harris escorted me outside to a limousine. I got into the limo by myself and the driver just took me on a drive around town by myself. All I could think of was the lesson that I learned in the bathroom, that a person is just a person and was grateful for the experience my mother allowed me to have and appreciated the limo ride. Later that year, Donna Gregory dropped off promotional items to my high school for my freshman ROTC class and donated funds to help with our military ball. I was able to go to her home and meet her family including a newborn baby and eat some of the best Italian food I have ever had.

Every year around Thanksgiving and Christmas I was tired of butter, flour, eggs, sweet potatoes, sugar and flour. My mother had me in the kitchen with her making numerous pies and cakes, then I did not get a chance to eat any of them. We would wrap them up and box them up and put them into her car and she would drive off with all of that sugary goodness in her car. When in high school, after bonding with Donna Gregory, my mother said "there are two sides to every story, would you like to see where the pies and cakes are going? Get your jacket come on let's get in the car." When we got to our destination and got out we approached a building that had hundreds of people in it. I started to talk to people and I learned that we were helping feed people that were homeless during the holidays. I met doctors, lawyers, teachers, preachers, and people from all levels of society, that things had just happened to.

A lot of the people I met were actually happy that we were there and opened up to me about their life and mistakes that were made or things that had happened to them. I learned so many powerful lessons this day. When we were leaving. my mother told me that all people deserve to be treated the same no matter where they are in life. We are all just people and my mother showed me this on both sides. Everyone deserves respect no matter where they are found in life. Successful or homeless we are human and some of us just need a little help every now and then, going back to the lessons her mother taught me of serving.

***

God sometimes sends us reminders along our path to let us know what direction we need to go in. I met one of his wise counselors in Rosalyn Dunlap Gentry, Esq. She is a remarkable mother to three sons and a loving wife to Howard Gentry, Founder of YBA (Young Blacks in Action), Author, Fitness Consultant, Speaker, Interior Designer, Business Consultant, Life Coach, Radio Host, and CEO. Author of bestselling book "The Power of Health", Six Time Division 1 Track & Field All-American; Two time Olympic United States Olympic Trials 400m participant. She set the World Record in 1982 Big 8 Indoor Championships in 600m with a time of 118.56 secs. She earned a BS in Housing and Interior Design '82 and a Master's in Business Administration '94, both from the University of Missouri-Columbia. She earned Juris Doctorate '05 from Florida A&M University School of Law. She motivates individuals to make positive changes to live a better life and to be of service to others. Believes we all are uniquely created for a specific purpose while living on this earth.

When I was a little girl, I always wanted to be an attorney. In 2013 I was blessed to meet a powerful Black female that was an attorney. I met this beautiful woman that lived my dream and was blessed and honored to be her administrative assistant at a Target Case Management facility in 2013. She reminded me that you really can do anything you put your mind to. A lawyer that has all these other talents and facets to her along with her extensive background, she stands in nothing but greatness.

One day I got the courage to ask her how and she taught me that we need to remove the blinders that society has placed on our culture, stop thinking that we are unworthy. She said "Ask God for what you want, work for it and towards it and you shall achieve it. We deserve not to live in poor neighborhoods, we deserve to acquire luxury experiences and that success is not restricted to ethnicity."

She taught me that anything can be negotiated and to create win-win solutions that help others become better or solve an issue that may be at hand. She allowed me to learn the importance of serving others with Mental Health solutions as well as becoming a marketing consultant for the firm. I also had the opportunity to learn about grant writing and case management notes and the importance of qualitative and quantitative data while in this position. She taught me that a Queen never steps off of her throne to respond to the negativity of others and to do everything with love and excellence. I am very thankful for the reiteration of the lesson that my grandmother and mother taught me and her allowing the creator to use her to speak through me and guide me.

Her lessons still stick with me to this day and will forever be in my heart. She has shown me that you can be successful in any and everything that you touch. When adversity comes your way use it as a steppingstone to get to something higher. I remember she told me once that if I ever make it, do not forget about her. Mrs. Rosalyn Dunlap Gentry I could never ever forget about you. Your lessons and presence in my life are embedded for you spoke to and nurtured my soul. You were a life coach to me without even knowing it. For that I am forever in your debt. Thank you.

***

As you read the words I have shared, I thank you for allowing me to share some of the lessons from people that have influenced me and I pray that these words pour into your soul and influence you in a positive way.

To those that have pushed me to walk in my purpose and impacted my life and legacy past present and future I thank you and I love you all. To our Creator above, I may not always understand what you are doing in my life but thank you for gracing me with your love and people that you have placed in my path to influence me, and those you have assigned to be influenced by me through you.

To my ancestors and those that came before me, thank you for allowing me to stand on your shoulders and making everything possible. Thank you for advocating for a better future so that I may be allowed to write such as this and more and obtain knowledge to assist with leading our culture into greatness. Thank you for your legacy, sacrifices, and guidance. To Dr. George C Fraser, Maya Angelou, and countless others. Thank you for using your voice and words and placing knowledge about our greatness and triumphs in books so that we may continue to rise and realize the greatness within us and our race for years to come.

To my Guardian Angels Teresa Carr, Josephine Campbell, and Ariana Carr. Thank you for the lessons that you taught me while you were graced to walk this earth alongside me, and the prayers and positivity that you poured into me while in this realm. Thank you for the protection and love you sent from the other worldly plane as you watch over our family and guide and protect us through God's Grace. You will never be forgotten.

To my best friend Tracy Goldston, Thank you for always being there to lift my head up when life gets hard and being there to encourage me and show me love no matter how long we may go without talking. I will love you always.

To Stan Matthews, thank you for taking me under your wing and providing the guidance of the father I never had. Thank you for seeing potential in me and praying over my life and my children's lives. I will be forever grateful for your wisdom, words, and kindness.

To Kim Bullock-Hennix, thank you for being strong and walking in your purpose and helping me realize mine. Your book , "The Birth of An Ambitious Woman" changed my life and what you wrote on the cover helped me simplify my purpose. To Uplift and Unite others. "Crown On" Queen.

To my children Alexis, Angelique, Ariana, Marquis, Elijah and Azariah. Thank you for being my children and being the beautiful beings that you are. I am not perfect and have made many mistakes in my life and you all have been nothing but inspiration for me to be a better person for you. I pray I make you proud. I am honored to be your mother and pray that the lessons this book brings you allow you to be fruitful and bring you encouragement, joy and direction and more throughout your journey. Make it a point to learn something new every day, pray and continue to evolve with grace and capture your insight. There is greatness within yo. Stand on the shoulders of our ancestors and never forget to dream, you can do anything you put your mind to and never ever forget that I love you and fight for you always.

To my grand babies Amir and Nadia and those to come, I love you always and pray and speak nothing but abundance and prosperity over your life and those that come from you. I hope this book will inspire, educate, equip, and propel you into your greatness.

Shanese Carr is a Mentor, Consultant, Visionary, Speaker, and upcoming Author of the Evolve-Capture Series. Shanese is dedicated to advocating for the dreamer in all of us, pushing us to dream and then design a blueprint or map to make them a reality. Her main purpose is to unite & uplift others.

She is the marketing consultant for the Southeast region of MBN (Matthews Business Network) the premier growth platform for established Black and Urban Business Owners, Professionals and

Non-profit Organizations, that has more than 2000 Members and associates in 12 regional chapters around the globe, including Asia, Africa, Europe, Latin America, and the Caribbean Region.

She is also the Owner and CEO of Elegance Enterprises, a unique development company located in Central Florida. They specialize in helping others get clarity on their professional vision and assist in designing innovative products, services & experiences to capture the attention of those who need them.

She is the Creator and Founder of the Evolve Capture Media Network, KQE (Kings & Queens of Elegance), The Collective, KQE Legacies, The Evolve-Capture Society as well as the publications KQE Magazine & Evolve-Capture Magazine. *She believes that we all have "the power to reinvent ourselves, to change our futures and to powerfully influence the rest of all creation." One of her favorite quotes by Dr. Stephen R. Covey.*

PATRICK CARTER

FAITH, EXCELLENCE, PROFESSIONALISM

PART I: FAITH – MRS. HELEN HAMLETT

I knew I was being fed a stream of lies from the very beginning, and now I was finally going to get some straight answers. Whole chunks of the story simply made no sense and everyone I spoke with was clearly in on this monumental fraud. Finally, I was going to be able to speak to the one woman my friends assured me would give me the answers I was looking for.

When we were kids, my parents worked, studied, scrimped, and saved to purchase a modest three-bedroom home in the suburbs of Newark, N.J, and around the corner was the Methodist church that dozens of southerners like my parents attended. It became their central place of worship, and there, they set roots.

My brother and I joined kids from other young church families, and through Sunday programs and activities, a coterie of children became bonded for life.

For many of us, Sunday School was better than real school, because from first to eighth grade the only book used was the Good Book. By the time we got to the 7th grade, we learned and could recite all the major stories, but I was starting to have problems with a lot of the "information" in that textbook.

We learned how God created everything in six days and how Noah built the ark to survive the flood. We were well-versed on the various exploits of Moses and the Chosen People. We were taught the life and times of Jesus Christ – all four versions, and we were informed about how it will all end in death and destruction, and for a precious, selected few, they will ascend unto glory in the arms of the returned Savior. *I just wasn't buying it.*

I was a child of science, of provable facts. I knew about dinosaurs, astronomy, the speed of light and carbon dating. I also knew there were many other religions full of good people who did not believe all these stories either. There was so much conflicting data and none of my science or math teachers would attempt to answer my questions on reconciling Sunday School and Grammar School.

My brother, who was three years older than me, and who was in high school, was not struggling with these questions. In fact, his private, parochial school had religious classes alongside the math and hard science classes. He could appreciate my pre-teen crisis of faith, so he told me, "Calm down. Just wait until you meet Mrs. Hamlett."

Mrs. Helen Hamlet, all five feet and one inch of joy; full of elegance, wisdom, and a woman who courageously volunteered to lead the Sunday School class for high school students. She grew up in the South and survived Jim Crow. She organized, protested, and fought for Civil Rights, battled housing and employment discrimination and, in her retirement; still had the God-given grace to work with children like us.

Her class was to "Sunday School" what NASA was to the Wright brothers. So, on my first day I introduced myself and unloaded five minutes of facts that proved the Bible was nothing more than a stack of lies! Mrs. Hamlett, armed with patience, experience, an unmovable faith and a laugh of pure joy was more than ready for the likes of me. Her response to my relentless rebuttal was: "God can do all things, including, handle your questions," she said to me with a smile on her face.

Over the next years, Mrs. Hamlett taught us what I called *practical* faith, one anchored in scripture, but not beholden to it. A faith that offered the example of Daniel to give young people the courage to face Bull Connor in 1963 and protest police misconduct in Minneapolis in 2020. She explained how we, like the Good Samaritan, could and should put the scripture into actions. She showed me that there is a difference between a lie and a lesson.

She taught all of us that there was no way we could grow, in faith or in life, without questioning and seeking answers. To this day, I marvel at the latest technical and scientific breakthroughs and recognize how they push a literal interpretation of the Bible into a smaller and smaller box, while at the same time, I am in awe of how the truths taught in those lessons become increasingly relevant and important with each day we live and each challenge we face.

PART II: EXCELLENCE – PAUL KNOX

Across the room, our eyes locked. The moment he recognized me anger registered on his face, and he started pushing through the crowd, making his way directly toward me. I was hoping I would see him before he saw me to avoid this exact situation. No such luck. He had seen me and now there was no way out.

My parents were born and raised in Alabama and Georgia, and they both believed and lived the power of education. The two of them traveled to the north armed with hope, work ethics, a place to live with family and "separate but equal" high school diplomas. They went on to earn associate, bachelor and master's degrees. On the foundation of that education, they were able to move past menial jobs, become medical professionals and were able to have a home, raise a family and live a comfortable life.

They spent the money to send us to the best private parochial (read: predominately white) schools during the week. Even for us kids, our refuge was coming back together with our Church family every Sunday to reconnect and recharge. I especially looked forward to the fourth Sunday of each month. On that Sunday, the regular "old folks" choir sat on the side while the younger, more exciting Modern Gospel Ensemble (MGE) led by Paul Know sat behind the minister and led the congregation in song. Paul Knox was a generation younger than our church's regular organist and cool. His level of excellence was so high that he played the church's huge pipe organ, the baby grand piano, and even brought in his electric keyboards. He could play all the old spirituals and the contemporary gospel songs we heard on the radio. Under his leadership, The MGE was so popular, all the kids wanted to sing with Paul. And luckily for us, there were only two requirements for entry: you had to be in high school and you had to bring your report cards to stay in the choir.

As choir director, Paul was a surrogate-everything to us. He was available when we needed a father, a brother, a minister, a doctor, a guidance counselor, a financial adviser, a counselor, a mentor, or a friend. He and his wife had all the children they could ever want with all the MGE kids, and for those of us MGE kids, the expectation of excellence was straightforward: spend four years in high school, get great grades, go off to college, graduate then come back to join the church as an adult member of the Ensemble. Occasionally, people veered from the plan in acceptable ways, like my brother did when he enlisted in the Army. Some people even extended the plan to five or six years over multiple universities, but the expectation never changed.

When I came home early from college after only six semesters, with two changes in majors but no degree and no focus, I knew I had veered too far from the accepted path. Carrying the weight of my mother's confusion, anger, and disappointment, I needed to regroup, reassess and recharge. I needed to go to church on Sunday---a Sunday that was on a fourth Sunday, a modern gospel ensemble Sunday, and a Paul Knox Sunday.

I had hoped to hang out on the balcony with the high school kids, listen to the sermon and sneak out before the end of the services, but when man plans, God laughs. The pastor opened by welcoming me back from college, and the entire congregation turned in unison to say hello, including Paul from his position behind the baby grand. With that friendly "hello," all hopes I had of escaping unnoticed were dashed.

After the sermon, Paul caught up with me, and after looking me over. I expected that Paul, like most people in my life at the time, would see a lost and broken 21-year-old, waiting for the latest barrage of unforgiving questions and dispiriting answers, but Paul surprised me. He took a moment before leveling one of his trademark statements-as-question: "I'm going to see you at Tuesday's rehearsal, right?"

With one sentence he gave me a first step, which would become a direction toward change that needed to happen in my life, and the beginning of a plan. Over the next few weeks, with Paul's help, direction, and unique support, I realized that my world was not ending, for he taught me that effectively managing failures is a vital component in life's overall success. I learned that excellence is not a destination, but excellence is a methodology, a mindset that drives you to get up when you are knocked down, and it keeps your bloody head unbowed. Excellence is the expectation Paul Knox taught me to always live up to.

PART III: PROFESSIONALISM – WALTER K BOOKER

The work of a sales professional is hard. The work of selling financial services – financial planning, insurance, mutual funds, stocks, bonds, etc. – is even more challenging. Contrary to the movie depictions, selling involves weeks of studying to pass state and federal licensing exams then the demanding work of learning specific strengths, weaknesses and benefits of each product and service. All of that work in pursuit of being seen as a professional who can be trusted to grow and protect a client's assets.

This is the world I chose to enter in the late 1990's when I joined MetLife Insurance. By this time in my life, I was accustomed to being one of only a few People of Color in the room, but in the financial services industry's lack of diversity was on a different level. From interviewing to training, the management to the clientele, this game was about the growth and preservation of wealth of overwhelmingly white clients.

I wanted to bring these important financial products and services to the Black and Latinx communities, where they were desperately wanted and sorely needed. To this end I signed up for more interviews, testing, licensing, and product training to take my talents to a company then known as American Express Financial Advisors.

Once inside, I had heard talk of a high-ranking leader, someone our director reported to, and someone who got his MBA from Harvard and knew everything about the business cold. A Black man who had the respect of every manager and financial advisor in the agency. I needed to do whatever I could to meet him one day. Until then, back to the grind.

While studying one day, a middle-aged Black man walked in the room and introduced himself as Walter. From his tailored suit, briefcase, and professional demeanor, I assumed he was one of the more powerful financial advisors managing hundreds of millions of dollars of client assets. He asked us how we were settling in, how we were working on our business and wished us well.

Later that day my manager called us to the conference room where he formally introduced Walter K. Booker, Group Vice-President, who spoke in front of our group about the company, the industry and trends we needed to be aware of, and he showed why he had both the title and the respect. Walter demonstrated that People of Color can rise to prominent levels in financial services, and I wanted to do what I needed to elevate my performance.

A few days later at a much larger meeting, held at one of the local private golf clubs, Walter spoke again, at times repeating – *word for word* – parts of what he said to the group in our office. I caught up with him after the meeting and joked that we must have been his guinea pigs. He paused and asked "Would you go into a prospect meeting cold, with no preparation or game plan? If you had the opportunity to role play with your manager, wouldn't you?"

With that, Walter helped me realize that to be at the top of the game at every level requires both preparation and hard work – two key ingredients of professionalism. Even today, after many more meetings, years, companies and industries, Walter shows that being a true professional means voluntarily doing the work others avoid. It means knowing both the data and, more importantly, knowing that it is people who generate it.

PART IV – WHO I AM

Beyond the quiet, demonstrated love of my no-nonsense father, the driven, success-focused adoration and unwavering support of my mother, I was blessed to have amazing people come into my life. It truly does take a village to raise a child, and I have dozens of lessons from so many village elders I cannot begin to list them all.

However, these three, Helen Hamlet, Paul Knox and Walter Booker have a special place for me. Combined were in my life for fewer than a dozen years, the majority well before my 20th birthday. Despite the relatively short time I got to spend with them, the outsized impact they had on me is both incalculable and still accruing.

From Paul I learned that my situation is the result of my actions. While it is easy to point fingers and blame the things that we do not control, it's harder and much more effective to look inward at what you DO control and work on those things.

From Walter I learned that, as a Black professional, it is equally important to see as it is to be seen. Walter's career at the time placed him in rooms with very few People of Color, from Ivy League classrooms to the top rungs of the financial services industry. His words of encouragement down the ladder of success gave me the drive to make my way through doors he was able open.

Mrs. Hamlet taught me through words and deeds that faith does not need a building or an official in pretty robes to be real and that God works through each of us to make this a better world. As (very) young adults, she challenged our child-like faith and encouraged us to question the things in our world that we did not understand. Only now, four decades later, one beautiful wife and two remarkable and extraordinary children later do I fully understand how valuable her lessons were.

THREE FOUNDATIONAL BUILDING BLOCKS: FAITH, EXCELLENCE. PROFESSIONALISM.

With these building blocks, you can, like I have been able to, walk confidently into new roles and opportunities, have the confidence that you are the right person in the right seat at the table and perform at levels well above par. I have been able to do all of this and more because that is what I have come to expect from myself as repayment to the remarkable people who influenced me.

Patrick Carter *is a retail sales leader who has built a 35-year career helping high-performing sales professionals recognize their full potential and also help his clients to discover new paths to success. He specializes in coaching, mentoring, training, and developing salespeople and sales leaders, and his podcast appearances, interviews, and scores of published articles are influential resources in a rapidly changing sales environment. Mr. Carter lives in New Jersey with his wife Julia, who he has been married to for more than 30 years. Together, they enjoy spending time with their children Kendall, Kierstan, and Bianca.*

SHIRLEY CARAWAY-BROWN

YOU ARE GOING TO COLLEGE

Mr. Stafford

Though more than a generation has passed, I can remember like it was yesterday. The stench of embalming fluid, Science class at Mechanic Arts High School. It was also the moment the trajectory of my life changed. It was late Spring 1974. It was my junior year and I was mercifully being saved by the bell and our frog dissection assignment. Entering the crowded hallway still clearing my nose, I rounded the corner and began climbing the stairs. If you lived through those times you remember the apple hats, bell bottoms, platforms, and afros that dominated the era. If you did not live through it, movies like Cooley High and Claudine reflect the urban experience and inner-city school dynamics of the era. Our hallways were always crowded, but as a soon to be rising senior I now navigated them with ease between classes. Out of the corner of my eye on the landing above, I noticed two Black male teachers chatting as they monitored passing time. It was a little strange because it seemed like they were waiting for me. As I reached the landing, a big smile emerged on Mr. Stafford's face. "You are going to college!" Confused, I looked around to see who he was talking about because he most definitely was not talking to me. "Yes, I am talking to you." Then he looked me straight in my face. And he said it again louder: "Shirley, I am talking to you. Yes, YOU, are going to college." Then again more slowly for emphasis "YOU ARE GOING TO COLLEGE!"

From that point on the world opened to me. There was a plan for me: I WAS GOING TO COLLEGE. After that I began working with Mr. Stafford, my American History teacher. He happened to already be my favorite teacher and he taught my favorite subject. We were going to make it happen. He had a plan to construct new history–new life stories–through myself and others that years laters could be looked to for inspiration. It was a different type of history– it did not start with what others agreed had happened. It started with a bold vision of the story I was going to be able to share: I WAS GOING TO COLLEGE–Not just what happened for me and others, but how we got it done.

Getting it done did not mean I understood the plan. It meant committing with everything I had to make it come true. It also meant absorbing instruction, direction, correction and wise counsel. I did not understand why he was doing it, how it would get done or even why he thought I could do it. There certainly was not what folks called a "college pedigree". No one I knew had gone to college–no one in my family, none of our family-friends nor anyone in the narrow circle of our community. We were everyday people doing ordinary things. I had solid grades, but I only had a few more As than Cs. I worked, looked after younger siblings and had an extracurricular sport or activity lined up for every season. I was a hurdle runner in the Spring, a feisty basketball guard in the Winter and a Fall/Winter cheerleader. Far fewer Black women in those days were attending college. The exit lanes were pretty much work, marriage or college. So with a young son on the way I did not fit the mold of the typical college-bound young lady of the 1970s. Nevertheless, I embraced the vision. My mind was focused on the goal. I committed to doing the work.

Hurdle One: make the time and show up. I came to Mr. Stafford's classroom after school. I know others were presented with the opportunity, but by the start of senior year only one student joined me on The Plan. The Plan became my new hobby and after school activity; track, basketball, cheerleading and much or the rest fell away. He selected the targets, chased the paper applications and kicked off the process by contacting the University of Minnesota and many Historical Black Colleges and Universities (HBCUs) on my behalf. Mr. Stafford worked with me to fill out every application and send them off. I recall never paying for postage to mail the applications or paying any application fees. I was never asked to pay and could not have paid for any of it if asked. He negotiated fee waivers on my behalf: He spoke with other teachers so that I secured recommendation letters. Those recommendations were a bigger commitment for teachers than they are today–they required executing perfect penmanship on a handwritten letter or a typewriter and an error-free typed letter.

Hurdle Two: select the "best" offer. After all that work, we waited and waited for the offers as the seasons changed. With all the work we put in I had not given much thought about what was to come next. Most of the schools were just names on a sheet. Some were more famous than others, but all were sight unseen. The exception was the University of Minnesota; it comfortably fit what I knew of the world and would require the least amount of sacrifices in my life and relationships.

The warmth of Spring was a reminder my senior year was coming to a close. So I said to myself "the U would be pretty great". Just as determined tulips suddenly emerged from the ground, the admissions letters arrived. I learned tulips and offers had a lot in common. Some tulips never rise, others leaf-out only and the best tulips rise with both leaf and bulb to full bloom. Despite my hopes, it became clear that the "U" was only going to leaf-out. The spring 1975 winner to my shock was the purple and gold bloom known as Prairie View A&M University (PVU). Although located in Prairie View, Texas (a world away and near-ly 1,500 miles from home) it was by far the "best" bloom of the season and the best fit. Of course that did not make it any easier to accept. It meant accepting that my future would be forged a world away. YOU ARE GOING TO COLLEGE would mean my future would not include the comforts of home, the life I had known, and easy access to the relationships most important to me. I had never traveled more than 50 miles from home or been away from my family for more than a week.

Hurdle Three: Go, keep going and finish the race with a kick. That year The Plan resulted in two fully-covered offers to

PVU, with a third to follow the next year. The Architect, Mr. Stafford negotiated for the University to cover our travel expenses, including a flight from St. Paul, MN to Houston, TX. We were writing a new story and called to construct a new history. When we stepped on campus and found the Yard, we stepped into a different world with the confidence that scholarships and books dedicated to us awaited. Mr. Stafford's vision elevated my conception of what was possible and called me towards the greatness buried within. The experience totally changed my life. It also prepared me to walk with excellence and created a strong sense of awareness throughout my PVU experience. I always knew Why and What I was doing there: People believed in me, I had no time to play (this was serious because I was being counted on to succeed).

My first day was full of firsts; it was both a promotion and a realization of how little I had known, done or experienced. As I entered the dining hall my mouth flew wide open: the aromas of the South, all kinds of shades of Black, the energy of youth all packed into one place. Of course while I understood PVU was a place of higher learning, I was in the midst of an experience touching all of my senses. After all, my worldview was framed from St. Paul, MN and this was an HBCU. The magnitude of the Black, intelligent, and proud people and my proximity to them was not the same. I was both amazed and caught off guard. Students were called from across the globe to attend PVU and we were asked to promote and advance change. Although I did not understand it fully–I knew this was a new beginning, an awakening. I would come to learn that knowledge is power and this power provides options. As I exercise my options, opportunities emerge that are unexpected, sometimes overwhelming and often hold great value. At the time I could not totally understand this foundational truth.

My vision had to be refined along the way. As my experiences expanded, my view of what was possible also widened and as an outcome my standard–the thing that I desired and expected from myself–rose. The vision went from: I am going to college (a college, any college) to going to PVU to being at PVU to graduating from PVU with a Mechanical Engineering degree. Each refinement of the vision brought new hurdles and sacrifices but the process was the same one I learned in high school. The intensity of the PVU experience was truly like no other. All the sleepless nights, studying groups, cramming for tests, camping-out in the Engineering Building–it laid a foundation of knowledge. While I believed knowledge and learning was anchored in critical Engineering concepts and calculations it was also the knowledge and learning about myself, my capacity and capability that made the sacrifices well worth it.

Oh! Don't get me wrong, it was not easy. In fact, it was one of the most difficult things I have ever done. The study of Mechanical Engineering in a degree program requires dedication and great focus. Engineering requires a solid understanding of science and math principles, and mastery of the ways those principles can be used both conceptually and practically to make life easier. For four years my schedule was packed, and I had to study consistently with little to no breaks. I wouldn't have traded experience and hold no regrets. I saw the vision: Bachelor of Science in Mechanical Engineering. I knew the process: make the time, show up and select the best course. I embraced my Why: maximize the options and opportunities so that my son and I had the best options for our life and future. There was no option to stop, quit, or give up.

Looking back there were a lot of funny moments along the way. When I would tell people that I was majoring in Mechanical Engineering most people, especially during college, thought I wanted to become a railroad engineer on a train and did not mind wearing a blue cap, overalls and being covered in grease or dirt. We have come a long way from many of those associations. There is a better understanding of the variety of ways engineering shapes our lives. There are more women and Black people in engineering and the hard sciences. There are many more Black women at HBCUs graduating from Engineering programs and enjoying successful careers. These advancements are due to those, who others did not always see as engineers, becoming engineers and committing themselves to shaping history to a more accurate narrative. They proved with skill and excellence that they could do the same job, in most cases with more qualifications and experience for the job, and complete to an equal or higher standard.

We were called into this rich legacy at PVU. It permeated from each professor's course and expressed itself in lectures, review sessions and assignments. Understanding that larger meaning and significance was utterly priceless. It further fueled the pursuit of my degree. Please don't assume this was expressed in friendly, collegial tones. Far from it they pushed us without fail and sometimes they pushed us very hard. Their courses required mandatory labs three days a week to ensure we immediately applied the principles taught to lecture to enhance our hands-on technical skills and enrich our critical thinking. It was a vital developmental tool. But I initially resisted thinking it "surely cannot take all of this". I quickly caught it and the kick propelled me forward. It really did take all of that to produce a PVU engineer! From thereon, I could work on almost any of the challenges put in front of me with greater ease. There was a natural flow. It was like poetry in motion or playing a beautiful melody. All the work and training came together in perfect harmony, simply because we refused to quit. I would not quit and many of us were encouraged to never give up. We kept trying, pushing forward, and would not stop. Buried deep was the promise I learned: Always remember WHY I was there: my mission was to finish; If I put in the work I will succeed; Achieving the dream produces options and rewarding opportunities.

From GOING to BEING to FINISHING I learned lifetime lessons. The strong, long-lasting friendships formed then are those I value until this day. The time, talent and treasures that were refined to graduate from PVU as a Mechanical Engineer have lasted a lifetime. As I matured, I discovered the importance of teamwork within the framework of an affirming traditional culture. Today, PVU continues to produce young Black and

Black female engineers at one of the highest rates in the nation. And I am proudly one of them. I FINISHED THE RACE.

THE ARCHITECT'S PLAN WORKED. His vision and our investment paid off. Two out of the three students who answered the call graduated from PVU with a BSME. I was the first and the only female student to do it. I am forever grateful.

MY GRANDMOTHER

Vera D. Caraway, my grandmother, was a force all her own. She is the woman who by and large raised me as I lived with The Trio (her, my great aunt Vena and my great grandmother Maddie) during my formative years. My mother was woefully unprepared to be a mother given her youth and her longings to fully explore life. My younger sister and I did not see much of her in those years as she fought to recapture the lost freedom of youth. She tried to regain it by running pillow-to-post while traveling from coast to coast.

For many years she expressed how much of a favor she did everyone. She would express it almost in heroic terms. For many years, I thought her attitude on the topic (abandonment, living her best life, rolling like stone) was selfish and delusional. Now when I think of my Granny, I believe we would have never formed the bond we had without the time and experiences we shared during those years. Granny, my grandmother, stepped into the void like many others did in those days when a barely mature child birthed a child of her own.

I believe she saw the pain and hurt of a young girl who felt like she was left behind, forgotten and had little value, worth or purpose. In those years she endeavored to love me and my little sister with all that she had—to share every piece of the wisdom she gained and provide a strong foundation for a greater purpose and meaning for life.

Granny, as a rule, barred my mother from keeping us until she showed she was responsible and had a stable life (predictable work, a place to live, solid relationship) in place. She stood up, stepped-in and protected us from what would have been a chaotic, unmoored childhood; I lived with Granny and the rest of The Trio until I left home for college.

The rhythm of life and the interactions between children and adults in those days was far different than what we see today. Phrases like "a child shall be seen and not heard" were a real part of everyday life. It was a standard for decorum in public and behavior at home; it was the clear line of demarcation between adults and children.

"A child (with a long pause)..." Granny would begin as a cautionary statement. Without uttering the rest of the sentence we knew what it meant: "Girl. Collect yourself, and get up out of this room, Right Now! Can't you see that grown people are talking?" It also meant to move without hesitation. As soon as I heard "A child..." I would finish the statement as a reply by responding on queue: "...shall be seen and not heard." Immediately I then collected myself in ladylike fashion and I left the room quickly. There was no back-talk, requests for understanding or demand for attention to my needs. There was also none of the back-and-forth interaction seen commonly today. It was simple. I moved. I followed the instructions. The rule trumped any need to understand the "why" behind it. Children were not allowed to sit in the room while adults were talking. Never. Ever. Period.

Granny also linked her code for conduct to the words children could not say under any circumstances. The biggies were "haa" and "what" in response to a request, question or instruction. Answering with things close to these phrases would truly irritate her. Now she would try to help you to get it right. The best response was: "Yes Ma'am", but "Yes" was also acceptable. The concept she drove home was that there was a proper way to address her and acknowledge any request. Of course, if I were so bold to answer her with "uh-huh" or a phrase like that she would just continue to call my name, as if she had not heard me, until I acknowledged properly.

Being raised by Granny, I found myself following the same tactics as a parent to my children and now as a grandmother to their children. "Yes" is an affirmative response and rarely raises ire; responding with "what" is a slippery slope. "What?" done with tone or abruptly is often disrespectful; without tone it may also communicate that you are questioning the validity of the request. Similarly, "haa" may communicate a lack of attention. Lack of clarity creates space for interpretation and misinterpretation and can influence the flow of any conversation. So I found a lot of wisdom in her approach. While I do not know why she would not allow it, hearing it from others irritates me too. Years later I learned Toastmasters International had a similar view of these unneeded filler words. It may be old school or it may just be my Granny in me, but children are not little adults, they need to be shielded from adult conversations, they need to be loved, cared for and treated like children.

Granny was one of those ordinary everyday people who had an extraordinary heart, a quick wit and loads of wisdom. She stayed home, kept a clean house, always made sure that we had a hot meal, combed our hair, made sure we had clean clothing and most importantly she kept a roof over our head. We were not well off, but I never remember really lacking too much for anything we needed. If there was a need The Trio made sure it was met. They worked together as a team to make sure that my sister and I were well taken care of until my mother found herself. "Did she find herself, yet?", was one of those lingering questions left unanswered during my youth; we were all hoping that someday she would be found.

My grandmother nurtured us and modeled an outstanding work ethic. She rose early and believed in taking the time to get things done right, the first time. Granny hated going back over something and redoing again. I found myself amazed as I watched her get the needed things done with a determined persistence and focus on the outcome. Either it got done or it did not get done. It was her true and sole metric of success. While she only had a 6-grade education, you had no way of telling based on the wit, quips and wisdom she offered. I carry many of her sayings with me: 1) You can lead a horse to water but you can't make him drink. 2) They lied on Jesus Christ. So why do you think they won't lie on you? 3) Baby! Let him know you are a live wire, then they won't step on you.4) Just like people have ass-holes they have opinions.

Because she stepped-up and stepped-in willingly I was positioned to meet the world with grace and inner strength. She would be the first in line to let you know if she thought you were not in the right, but she would do it in love. Granny was the glue of our family and kept all her grandchildren together. It was not an easy task reasoning my mom and aunts who were not always receptive to her voice or doing "good enough" for their children. There were times that we all lived in one house–my Granny and all 15 of her grandchildren.

Sundays were always special in my grandmother's home. She woke-up a little earlier than usual to prepare and place Sunday dinner on the table. Like clockwork everything was prepared and ready to be eaten at 2:00pm without fail. On the Sunday of your birthday week, she baked a yellow cake with chocolate frosting and placed a number on it for your birthday year. The birthday girl always received the honor of selecting the menu. I also cannot omit sharing the deliciousness of my Great Grandmother's peanut butter frosted cakes. Her cake and hearing her voice every Thanksgiving saying, "Baby! Don't you put too much nutmeg in that pie, it will make it bitter," is something I will never forget but always miss.

Granny was an excellent cook, but was not one to measure. She measured nothing. This made it a little difficult when it came time for me to make Thanksgiving dinner. She offered a lot of "taste it as you go and you'll know when it is enough". When I directly asked "How many eggs do you put in a sweet potato pie?" Her response was "It should be like a custard, but beat them in one at a time." Again, that did not tell me much. Since then I have done the same.

As you can imagine with the cooking, love and family our house became the hangout spot. Our house was always full of my cousins and friends. This also meant that if you were late getting home on time for dinner there would be nothing left for you to eat that night. Sometimes my cousins and their friends would eat up everything. One time I remember I was left with a bone left in a big empty pot of beans.

Now I continue the legacy of my Granny. I'm here to help guide, nourish, protect and push my children, grandchildren and the generations to come onward to their own greatness. I am here to help them focus and discover their worth, know their value, and deepen their destiny. The circle has been rounded now the child has become the grandmother. I truly did not realize it, but there was and is a purpose and meaning to it all and I thank you Lord for showing me the way through each of our experiences.

TERRENCE

My husband Mr. Terrence Sr. is an awesome partner. He is always dependable, reliable and the greatest plus to my life. He is my rock and has always supported all my endeavors. We have forged a loving partnership and friendship. We have raised four great children and we are in the process of helping to raise our twelve grandchildren and one great grand-daughter (at the time of printing). I fully anticipate the family will continue to grow and know the legacy will continue. We met at Prairie View A&M University one summer evening in September. We dated for four years and have been married for forty-two years coming this May 2022. People often ask me the same question: "How do you stay with the same guy for so long?" There really isn't a magic answer. I have learned to just keep falling in love with him over and over again. I work hard not to hold onto situations for long periods of time when we differ.

Whenever I am away from him for any period of time I just do not feel right. I still hardly sleep when my husband is away on work trips,I still.. It just feels just a bit off and I toss & turn most of the night. Once his feet hit the door, I can go straight to sleep because he is back home. It's that type of bond, that type of love. Terrence brings the stability of our family. He has been the anchor and my grounding. I grew up without my biological father in my life. However, Terrence has always brought leadership and foundation to our relationship.

Terrence is for the most part a very quiet person. To this day it is still hard to figure him out at times. He can be extra quiet; it's just how he is. There may be a link to him being 1 of 12 children and three oldest. When I consider his leadership, I believe he learned to lead his family from his father and the foundation of family from his mother. We stick and stay together no matter what. Family is the nucleus of a strong foundation and legacy for the Brown household. And so, it has impacted our family. We are stronger together. We build together and push for excellence in all that is connected to the family line. With love and persistence, we always seem to make it.

Thank you, Terrence! For teaching me how to pull it all together and how to push them all forward and to stay strong, steady, wavering but driving the ship straight and steady and anchoring her home. We shall see the fruits of our labor.

_____

Shirley Caraway-Brown is, a daughter, sister, mother, and wife. She is the oldest of five children. She was born in St. Paul, Minnesota. Shirley is a graduate from Prairie View A&M University BSME (first in her family). She is also seeking to complete her MMS. This scripture I hold dear because it was given to me by my spiritual Father:

> *Isaiah 45:1-6KJV Thus saith the LORD to his anointed, to Cyrus, whose right hand I have holden, to subdue nations before him; and I will lose the loins of kings, to open before him the two leaved gates; and the gates shall not be shut;[2] I will go before thee, and make the crooked places straight: I will break in pieces the gates of brass, and cut in sunder the bars of iron:[3] And I will give thee the treasures of darkness, and hidden riches of secret places, that thou mayest know that I, am the LORD, which call thee by thy name, am the God of Israel.[4] For Jacob my servant's sake, and Israel mine*

elect, I have even called thee by thy name: I have surnamed thee, though thou hast not known me.[5] I am the LORD, and there is none else, there is no God beside me: I girded thee, though thou hast not known me:[6] That they may know from the rising of the sun, and from the west, that there is none beside me. I am the LORD, and there is none else.

Shirley holds a position (supporting Information Technology /Quality) at a Major Medical Device Company and she assists at Swan Associates. Together with her son their combined experience holds over 40 years of Quality Engineering and Project Management experience. As they provide teams the correct tools to achieve Excellence.

Shirley and her husband have been married for 42 years (as of May 2022). She has four amazing children, twelve dynamic grandchildren and one great-grand daughter. That all challenge her to be at her best.

Proverbs 13:22 KJV A good man leaveth an inheritance to his children's children: and the wealth of the sinner is laid up for the just.

I am grateful for this opportunity to serve as the doors that were once closed are now opened.

DR. MARIE F. CELESTIN

PLANTING SEEDS OF FREEDOM: A LEGACY BIRTHED BY HAITIAN WOMEN

"Stories, whether within the family of folktales, or just spirituality and rituals, are so important to survival, to continuity... We're connected by our stories."
Edwidge Danticat

I am the celestial daughter of Haitian immigrants, raised by strong, hard-working, resilient women: my grandmother, affectionately named Idora, my mother, Jeannine Celestin, and my aunt, Marguerite "Tante Margot." I come from a lineage of liberators, freedom fighters, healers birthed by matriarchs who sacrificed themselves so I can live freely and fiercely, get educated to thrive wherever I go. I inherited their incomparable work ethic and strong will to excel despite life circumstances. Black excellence and wealth are my birthrights. I get to manifest my ancestors' wildest dreams because of their unshakeable resilience and courage.

I am a limitless being because of them.

I'm often asked indirectly and not so subtly, "Where are you from?" Depending on the day, I'll say where I currently live, where I was born, or give a vague answer. I discovered early on as a young woman that every room I enter and leave, I announce in silence a part of who I am. I describe myself as human first, daughter, sister, scholar-practitioner, poet, activist, multi-passionate creative, nurturer, and infinite learner. I'm Haitian-American, raised and educated in success in Boston, rooted in my heritage and the Afro-Caribbean diaspora. My aunt and grandmother raised my middle sister and me after my mother moved to the US. Years later, as preteens, we both immigrated to Boston to reunite with her. In retrospect, this is the first time I started feeling out of place and being treated unfairly as an exotic alien. The human thing to do as a girl then was to retreat and put on a mask until I piece myself back together. As an introvert, books were my sanctuary and made me feel connected to a bigger world beyond my neighborhood. Being a book lover even led me to my first after-school job in a neighborhood library. Every experience, relationship, and community is connected to my evolution as a Haitian-born girl discovering myself, my voice, purpose, and place in this world.

Boston is the first U.S. city I ever lived in and put down roots there for my family, education, professional career, and growing community life. Although, it took me years to get acclimated to living in a cold caste-like city with little sunshine, palm trees, and mangoes. The first few years, I missed everything about living on an island surrounded by people who look like me and speak the same language. My yearning for home led me to my first loves, poetry, and music. I was immersed in the written words and lyrics to make sense of what I was going through and a heightened level of isolation even surrounded by family. I had no one to express the depth of my home-sickness. At home, my mother primarily spoke Haitian Creole. Back then, I wrote in both French and English as I was still learning the new language. I was constantly translating everything in my head before speaking at home and at school. I poured my heart out on paper about everything that I couldn't say aloud. It's what I call poetic storytelling, the intentional and sacred habit of writing about my lived experiences. My love of words helped me find wonder, comfort, and safety between the pages of my favorite books.

As I get older, I recognize the power of cultivating intentional community and chosen family. I've been fortunate to have had many invaluable mentors, advisors, supporters, and friends who saw the potential in me before I did. The lessons they taught are priceless and more relevant as I grow more into who I am. I didn't realize how much they taught me until our lives were disrupted by geography, modern-day busyness, or tragedy. I'm grateful for their guidance and lessons learned that continue to help me navigate this ever-changing world.

In addition to my newfound community, I learned the most memorable lessons from my family. My grandmother and aunt taught me about unconditional love and what it means to feel safe and belong. As strong and brave Haitian women, they were inherently selfless matriarchs, caregivers, nurturers, and providers who put the needs of their families and communities first. Their sacrifices despite danger and struggles, paved the way for every member of our family to have a better life in Haiti and abroad.

My grandmother, affectionately called Idora, treated me like an angel, her angel, who can do no wrong in her eyes. She beamed with joy every time I walked through her home and spent time with her. Like many women of her generation, she birthed more than ten children and raised more than 20 grand-children. Her home in Haiti, although modest, was always filled with family, friends, and children from the neighborhood. She was either at home cooking, sewing, gardening, at church, or at the market selling goods from her garden. She inspired my love of plants and to grow my own food. Since our kitchen was outdoors, no food scraps were wasted. As she prepared vege-tables to be cooked, she would throw the seeds in one area of our backyard. I was in awe just watching her in her element. She seemed the happiest while humming her favorite songs, harvesting the fruits of her labor, and then feeding us and the whole neighborhood.

Despite always being surrounded by children and family members, she made me feel special just being my shy self. Her love for me was manifested on a plate of rice and beans, fried plantains, and pork "griot" with pikliz. I missed those treasured moments with her after I immigrated to America, our closeness was not diminished by distance and the years we spent apart. Sadly, I never saw her again until I returned to Haiti for her funeral. Despite her transition, there is a deep knowing that I'm still her angel and she is mine watching over me. Every time

I'm in my own garden now, especially when tending to my vegetables and flowers, I can feel her near.

Similar to my grandmother, my aunt made me feel wanted, like one of her children and a rightful member of her family. Her non-negotiable expectations of me were to get good grades in school, respect my elders and stay out of trouble. As long as I followed those rules while under her roof, I remained her beloved daughter-niece. She was intentional in treating me and my sister like we were her own. In addition to being a mom and aunt, she was a registered nurse and an entrepreneur ahead of her time. Back then, she still wore the official white nurse uniform with the cap and shoes to match. Although she worked long hours and often came home exhausted after her shifts, she was proud of her professional achievements. In hindsight, she was the first woman in our family with a side hustle alongside a full-time job.

One defining quality that we have in common is her strong work ethic and commitment to the well-being of her people. She worked five days a week at a local hospital in Haiti while raising four children, taking care of aging parents and other family members, and running her business. Besides being the primary breadwinner, she was also an active community member who enjoyed going to church. She lived faithfully and supported her extended family despite facing many adversities.

As an immigrant girl, there were, may still be the case today, limited career paths that encouraged me to become a nurse or teacher. I clearly understood my aunt's dedication to nursing but I'm not really sure she chose it. Watching her work so hard for years with barely any time for herself juggling family life, made me realize that nursing was not in my future. Plus, I didn't like the smell of hospitals and they made me think of death. Ironically, after college, I started working in the medical center as a Health Educator and quickly learned that there are many roles besides nursing and doctor in a hospital setting. Before she passed away, my aunt assured me that as long as I remain a student with a good job, and take care of myself and my family, I will make her proud.

Her spirit is still guiding me, especially during times of uncertainty. She taught me so many valuable life lessons that are still helping me navigate this ever-changing world. The first lesson is to trust my instinct and my quiet way of being. She recognized my love of books and encouraged me to stay curious and explore my academic interests. There are times I doubted myself and felt inadequate for not having all the answers. Through her guidance, I gave myself grace to define what success meant to me and pursue careers that were in alignment with who I wanted to become. It was important to me not to disappoint her after everything she has done for me, for us to have a better life in America. She gave me permission to make bold moves even when I was scared and trust my gut no matter what. Like my grandmother and those before her, she's been tested many times but she always bounced back and ensured she found a way to rise above her circumstances. I inherited her resilience and determination to grow through it all. I was born from a people and a country that fought for every ounce of freedom, women who risked everything to afford me the privileges to re-imagine a limitless future.

Similar to my grandmother and aunt, my mother's core values were her faith, family, and work ethic. She worked tirelessly and held multiple jobs until she became ill and was forced to retire early. I now keenly know the sacrifices that my mother made for me to be here and have access to more opportunities than she had. One of her favorite sayings was, "there is a season for everything." We've had many seasons where we struggled and other periods filled with special occasions like weddings and birthdays. Because of her, I became a non-profit founder, college graduate, serial entrepreneur, best-selling author, and wellness expert while making a positive impact in the world. Since her passing, the meaning of her favorite saying resonates with me more deeply.

Each day is sacred and a chance to start over with grace and gratitude. The lessons that I learned and now apply daily from my grandmother, Idora, tante Margot, and my mother, Jeannine will guide me for a lifetime. The values they instilled have molded me into the person I'm unbecoming and becoming to live a life by design in alignment with my divine purpose. Every day I'm strengthened by their spirit, memories, knowing they are always with me. Their collective influence has given me the power to grow seeds of freedom, my own legacy, and that of generations to come. I am infinitely possible because of them.

FAVORITE QUOTES

"I'm no longer accepting the things I cannot change. I'm changing the things I cannot accept." ~ Angela Davis

"Knowing how to be solitary is central to the art of loving. When we can be alone, we can be with others without using them as a means of escape." ~ Bell Hooks

Thank you to Mr. Stan Matthews and Dr. George C. Fraser for the opportunity to be a featured contributor in this amazing book. I'm grateful for the coaching, mentorship, and support that I've received from MBN. We truly are stronger when we work together.

I honor my late grandmother, mother, and aunt who raised me to believe in and tap into my limitless potential. To our good ancestors, foremothers, freedom fighters, truth-tellers, artists, and change-makers who paved the way for women like me to live freely, create boldly, and tell our stories authentically. The circle of friends, family members, teachers, healers, plant lovers, coaches, creatives, entrepreneurs, Second Life friends, light workers, and allies who have contributed to my success is too long to share their names here. You've inspired me to grow more into myself and share my innate gifts with the world. I'm no longer playing small and dimming light because I'm more grounded in who I am and fiercely affirm that I am here on purpose for a purpose.

To Maxm, the love of my life, you're my epic WHY for dreaming bigger and creating an abundant life as part of our legacy. A special acknowledgment to my sisters, Cassandre and Christine who are building their legacy on their own terms. Like the phenomenal women who influenced me, I admire their determination and work ethic. Freedom in in our DNA.

I'm appreciative of two brave women who've been in my life since I was a young woman. The first is Kerline Augustin, my late mother's friend with a big heart, who lovingly checks up on me. She's always been kind to all of us since settling in Boston. She is one of my angels on earth who I can count on, especially after my mother transitioned.

I honor Gerthy Lahens, Founder of the Renaissance Project and long-time humanitarian and activist whose dedication to Haiti and its people is unparalleled. Her ability to galvanize people and courage to fight for justice for the Haitian community has inspired me to become a champion for equality. She has partnered with countless individuals and institutions across the globe to ensure Haiti is remembered and the people and culture are celebrated. As my beloved country, she too is a treasure to be revered.

I'm grateful for so many of you who have connected and reconnect with me, particularly during the pandemic. Words cannot express how much I appreciate you. To members of the GIRLS project, Boston While Black, HAMA, and HER Slayground HOC, and EwE community, you helped me amplify my quiet leadership to a whole new level. My inner circle has fortified my superpowers and purpose on this planet. I get to show you how to joyfully be well through the gift of putting yourself first unapologetically. I'm energized to see the next seeds we plant, grow and harvest together. Remember, you are worthy of all the goodness.

Dr. Marie F. Celestin *is a multi-passionate wellness coach, poet, and bestselling author of Planting Seeds: A Sacred Self-Care Journal. She's featured in 1 Habit to Thrive in a Post-Covid World. Dr. Celestin is committed to showing women the gift of putting themselves first unapologetically. She intentionally centers lived experiences, worthiness, healthy living, joy, and healing in her transformative coaching practice. She also teaches about the benefits of integrating plants into your wellness journey. She is working on her first collection of poetry. Her publications are available on Amazon.*

MARTIN DAVIS

LOVE, LEADERSHIP AND INSPIRATION

My Mentor George Grant

Oftentimes when I reflect upon the early years of my life, I recall that I looked forward to the holidays and summers hanging out with friends in the Coney Island neighborhood of South Brooklyn, New York. One of my favorite past times was going to the New York City Youth Services Agency (YSA), commonly referred to back then, as the Coney Island (CI) Youth Board. **George Grant** immediately comes to mind. Mr. Grant, no doubt was emphatically a person of significant influence in my life and that of many others whom he served while working as a youth counselor for the New York City Youth Services Agency (YSA), commonly referred to back then, as the Coney Island (CI) Youth Board. Upon his employment Mr. Grant formulated a club for young males in the elementary and Junior High School age group. The group known as the "Junior Archons" was in essence an extension of an existing group of teenagers lead by Mr. James C. Jones, Jr. (Director of the CI Youth Board) known as the Archons (a Greek word that means "ruler"). Mr. Jones used basketball as a tool to mentor young men through love, leadership, and inspiration. He taught them how to lead meetings, rise above their circumstances, and be well-respected leaders in their families and community. Mr. Grant also espoused these principles to cultivate the lives of youth under his charge. The three ways in which he personally impacted my life are 1) he demanded that I endeavor to enhance my knowledge and comprehension via exposure to various written bodies of work fiction, non-fiction, drama, and literature such as poetry; 2) he encouraged me to be a leader amongst my peers, in my community, society at large; and 3) to always remember that to whom much is given much is required.

Mr. Grant introduced members of the Junior Archons to the performing arts such theatrical productions. Some of my fondest experiences include live theatre performed by The Negro Ensemble Company at the Henry Street Settlement House where many notable members such as John Amos, Moses Gunn, Rosalind Cash, Sherman Hemsley, Roscoe Lee Brown, Esther Rolle, Glynn Truman, Clarice Taylor, and many others honed their acting skills. He also introduced a few of us to the musical art form Jazz when we experienced the live performance of a blind multi-instrumentalist Rahsaan Roland Kirk whom I was astounded to witness play three horns at once (a tenor saxophone, Manzello and Stritch as a basic part of his artistic expression - the manzello is essentially a B-flat soprano sax with a curved neck, a straighter pipe, and a upturned bell similar to the Saxello sold by the H. N. White Company from the mid-1920s until the late 30's; the Stritch is a similarly modded E-flat alto, but this time without the usual upturned bell). Rahsaan did so constructing distinct counter melodies, paying harmony for himself and pitting rhythm against rhythm at a weekend jazz club called "The East" located at 10 Claver Street in the heart of the Bedford-Stuyvesant neighborhood of Brooklyn, New York. During this performance he also played the flute, clarinet, and soprano saxophone. Another noteworthy artist that I recall performing that night was Pharoah Sanders. One summer he demanded that we do something constructive with our time, so we opted to take up photography. The program had a limited budget, but we were able to purchase a few cameras, rolls of 35-millimeter film, an enlarger to development the film in a dark room, the chemicals such as developer and fixer to develop film and print pictures. As a result of this summer project several individuals went on to become professional photographers.

Mr. Grant attended Graduate School at Long Island University and upon graduation became a public-school teacher. During his career he taught English and ultimately was named Vice Principal at Alexander Hamilton High School located in Brooklyn, New York where he continued his influential ways. At Hamilton, Mr. Grant worked with Mr. Raymond Haskins, who previously also was one of my mentors at YSA. Akin to Mr. Grant, Mr. Haskins was also one of the individuals that I endeavoured to emulate in my approach to giving back and leaving an indelible impact on the lives of individuals that I have ability to teach, support and protect in the workplace. I cherish the fact that these exemplary men and others such as Jerry Rodgers have impacted my life in a meaningful way.

OLDER SIBLINGS

In many respects my sister **Bernadette** was like a second mother to me. She is the oldest of my siblings and always seemed to exhibit a nurturing influential in my life. Bernadette, or Bonnie the name she was affectionately called by family and friends, was a young adult when I reached my teenage years. She graduated from the Nursing program at Clara Barton High School in Brooklyn, NY an began working as a Licensed Practical Nurse at Maimonides Hospital. A few years later she moved out on her own and got married. I looked forward to walking to her house to spend quality time with her during the late afternoon upon her arrival home from work. She would complete crossword puzzles from the daily newspaper while watching the soap opera "Dark Shadows" on television. When she gave birth to her first child Tahnee, and subsequently her second daughter Tasha, she demonstrated a maternal instinct that I always knew that she possessed as she had been protective of me as if I were her child.

Years later, Bonnie decided that it was time to enroll into college while still working in order to become a Registered Nurse (R.N.) as she had missed the widow period to apply and be awarded the R.N. designation based upon time in-service and experience. Thus, she attended and graduated from

Long Island University with a Bachelor of Science degree in Nursing. Going back to school many years later was no easy task for Bonnie, especially while working and raising a family; nevertheless is was necessary for her to obtain the professional status and pay that she deserved. I am most proud that Bonnie went on to become a Surgical Operating Room Nurse at both a New York City hospital, and a private affiliate, simultaneously, and was able to reture from

My sister **Josephine Theresa**, whom family and friends call Terry, is next in the line of my siblings. Terry was somewhat influential in my life during my early elementary school years as she insisted that I follow directions, be respectful and do well in school. Looking back as an adult I realized that the disciplinary aspect stems from an incident which occurred when Terry took me to the park and told me to stand in front of the fence while she swung on a swing. I didn't listen and walked around the fence and was struck by the corner of Terry's swing below my left eyebrow. That incident warranted that I be taken to the local hospital and receive ten sutures.

Some of my fondest memories are from times when I would travel from The Choate School in Wallingford, Connecticut to Penn Station located at West 34th Street in Manhattan, New York. Depending upon the time of day I would go to 2 Penn Plaza adjacent to Madison Square Garden and go to the Buck Consultants office to visit Terry. She and many of her colleagues were always happy to see me and would provide me encouragement regarding my academic pursuits. During those brief visits I had the opportunity to observe some sophisticated computer and key punch operations.

My third oldest sibling, **Diane,** has provided a steadfast influence in my life. When I was in elementary school, I was amazed that she routinely received ribbons, metals, plaques, and trophies for her academic and athletic prowess. She would win at track & field events; ping pong; spelling bees and scrabble tournaments. Additionally, she was a force to be reckoned with when she competed in local and regional singing competitions. Playing board, word and card games with Diane, and family members, fostered a friendly spirit of competition that remains engrained today. While playing scrabble, prior to making a triple word score using all seven letters, there would be a caesura as if she were speaking reciting poetry. Diane was a vocal artist and performed professionally with a band at the legendary Apollo Theatre in Harlem and other venues in the Northeast. She was offered a contract to become a solo artist but declined and stopped performing shortly thereafter.

Observing Diane's work as a public servant when she worked for the New York City Youth Board and later Youth Services Agency (YSA) in Coney Island provided a subconscious influence and motivation for me to later become a public servant. I saw first-hand the impact that she and her coworkers had on the youth that they served. In September of 2013 Diane was among several noteworthy individuals that were honored for exemplary community service at a Gala Celebration in Brooklyn, New York. I along with numerous others, including high ranking New York City officials, commend my Sister for her dedication and tireless continued service for over five decades, working for the City of New York, providing Senior Secretarial and Administrative functions for the Youth Board, YSA, Child and Family Service Agency, and the Administration for Children's Services.

Spencer, the fourth and last of my older siblings was my only brother. Spencer loved to sing   and would listen to music sung by the DELFONICS; DELLS; STYLISTICS; BLUE NOTES and other groups that inspired romance. My appreciation for love ballads was largely influenced from my brother routinely listening to these classic ballads and singing along with the records. Although Spencer was not thrilled with classroom learning he was able to acquire many skillsets and was influential to me as he demonstrated that anyone could learn to do anything from reading directions and following instructions on how to perform a task. He often told me if you have the proper tools and follow the instruction you can build or repair most things. Spencer was someone I could always count on and as a result emulated his best characteristics.

As a result of being skilled in the martial arts he earned the respect of several neighbor bullies and those who might routinely seek to cause conflict. During my preteen years Spencer was my tutelary. He taught me to never start trouble, but if a problem arose to seek ways to de-escalate the problem, but if it could not be avoided to defend myself. He would not allow anyone to disrespect him nor our family, otherwise he was the kindest and nicest person you could ever meet.

Among his many acquired skills and self-learned accomplishments, Spencer was a certified locksmith; certified to repair radios & televisions; a licensed notary republic and was skilled at Citizen Radio Band and shortwave communication. Spencer held occupations as an auto mechanic; an Armored Guard for Wells Fargo; a tow truck operator; and lastly a New York City Sanitation worker where he was employed long enough to retire with benefits. My brother who was well liked by his peers, coworkers and those who knew him transitioned to join the ancestors several years ago. I miss my beloved brother dearly and will continue to cherish his memory forever!

MY COUSIN RALPH

My cousin **Ralph Malone**, the eldest offspring of my mother's twin sister Mary, was considered by many to be quite sapient. He had an extensive vocabulary and was well versed in a plethora of topics including science, mathematics, history, world politics, literature, poetry, music and many others. He had an opinion and was armed with the facts to substantiate his rationale. Ralph was a consummate reader and was certainly one of the most articulate people that I have ever encountered in my entire life. Those individuals whom were well acquainted with him did not address him by his birth name of Ralph, instead they called him "DOC". At an early age I was influenced by Cousin Ralph because whenever I saw him, he usually had a book in hand. I would sit and listen to him converse with my father and others in the community, regarding a wide range of subjects, for seemingly hours at a time.

On fall and winter weekends during the mid 1960's Cousin Ralph would come to my house, go into a bedroom, close the door and watch the Syracuse University Football game on television. Syracuse was his favorite collegiate football team, and he did not want anyone to disturb him while he was watching the game. After a while I realized that this game of guys running up and down a grass field tackling one another was one of his favorite past-times. I now recall that I could neither pronounce the name of the college, nor understand the intricacies of the game of football. I was subliminally influenced by his unwavering support of this Upstate New York football team, and I wondered why he would periodically talk or shout out as if someone inside the television screen could hear him. Evidently, I was unknowingly influenced by his practice of verbal communication with an inanimate object as I have the tendency to exhibit this same behavior when watching any of my favorite sports teams on television.

Like several of his peers and young men of color living in inner cities (in general), during his formative years, Ralph got caught up in the errant ways of street life, was incarcerated and was remanded to New York State penal correction facilities. He served several months to several years away from his family on an occasion or two. As one would suspect he spent a lot of time reading while incarcerated and when released after his last bid he became a community advocate, worded and served on a community advisory board for youth. I had the distinct privilege of being one of a handful of teenagers to participate as a member an ADHOC group led by Raymond Brown and Ralph Malone. They taught us (the Youth) Robert's Rules of Law so that we would know how to conduct meetings and make decisions as a group. This was necessary training that would ensure that we could effectively interact and communicate with groups like ours, from other communities such as Crown Heights, when we attended several empowerment weekend conference trips.

Ralph or DOC, as I would refer to him when I became a young adult, influenced my life in ways that I am now just beginning to realize. If he saw me in the presence of a person or individuals that had unsavory reputations, he would admonish me. His words to me on those few occasions were don't be like me. He soon realized that I was a good judge of character and would not allow myself to get caught up in any negative activity or situation that could bring embarrassment or shame upon my family. I recall at least two times when he took me to one of his favorite shoe stores and purchased a pair of fine Italian shoes made by VERDE.

I had a special relationship with my cousin and was tasked by my Mother to locate him and inform him that his beloved Mother (Aunt Mary) had transitioned during the wee hours of that sorrowful morning. I would be remiss if I would forget to acknowledge that DOC was proud that I attended an elite preparatory school and went on to attend college at Syracuse University, as he held academics in high regard. The last time that I saw DOC I was unable to have an open conversation with him as I was accompanied by a friend of mine, Leonard, who was from Bedford Stuyvesant, Brooklyn, New York. At that time DOC told me that he would not be around much longer and that he would continue to live through me. Obviously, I was caught off guard by his assertion and I thought that he was just giving me the business as I had not seen nor reached out to him in a while. Instead of engaging him and conversing, I told him that I would be able to dialogue with him freely in a few weeks since I was planning to come home for a brief visit. To my chagrin that never came to pass as DOC transitioned from pancreatic cancer a few weeks later. In death as in life my Beloved cousin Ralph "DOC" Malone taught me that tomorrow is not promised for anyone and that we should not put off things that we can do today for a later date.

DEDICATION LOVE LETTER

This love letter of dedication affords me the opportunity to cover the spectrums of time in my life by reaching back to the past, observing the present and giving honor to those who will inhabit the future. I offer a prayer to honor those who have positively impacted and influenced my life.

Sincere appreciation, and thanks to my Mom Martha Davis, my Dad James Shivers, and the Creator, who gave me the breath of life. To all of my siblings, In-laws Dennis, Maureen, Lamont, Maurice and their families, my lifelong friends Lawrence and Baron Pack, Frank, and Barry Minor, Carzie and Alonzo Scales, Carleton Gordon, Ronald Stewart, Clarence Williams, Jerry Rodgers, Timothy Bradley, Sheldon Leary, Gregory Fields, Lemuel B. Wilson, Ronald Peek, Raymond Kotright, Stan Matthews, Ralph Henderson and many others.

Prayers of continued blessings to my beloved wife Michelle and our children Divinia, Martin-Abdul, Destiny, and Malcolm-Ali. I leave a prayer for prosperity and a legacy of success to you as well as grandchildren and great grandchildren yet unborn to maintain a connection from the ancestors of past generation on to future generation to come.

Martin Davis has 35 years of professional experience in occupational health and safety. He was an Occupational Safety and Health Specialist for the Department of Veterans Affairs at the Brooklyn VA Medical Center, and then transferred to the U. S. Department of Labor Occupational Safety and Health Administration (OSHA), where he served as a field Compliance Officer, an Assistant Area Director, and a Compliance Assistant Specialist. He later held roles as a principal consultant for HazTek Safety Management, Inc. and more recently with Med-Tex Services. At present, he is the Principal of Assured Safety Management, where he serves as a safety and health management consultant, conducts work site audits and program assessments, conducts accident investigations upon request, and provides OSHA subject matter instruction.

JOSE GONZALEZ

THE AGE OF INNOCENCE

I watched as the flight attendant closed the waist length blue chiffon curtain inscribed with the words "Pan Am". I turned to my Dad and inquired why she was closing the curtain. He told me it was to separate us from the smoking section, which I found ironic since the Marlboro clouds in our cabin were thicker than the cumulus clouds outside my window.

Soon after, the flight attendant returned, pushing a cart down the aisle and asking the passengers, "Chicken or Beef?" As a 7yr old, I was quite the school lunch aficionado. I was used to eating on compartmentalized cardboard trays but these trays were made of hard plastic. There was a soft dinner roll with a butter packet, a Frenched chicken breast smothered in a delicious gravy, mashed potatoes, green beans and a mouthwatering brownie. As much as I loved those school lunches, this was true culinary artistry! My Dad wasn't as impressed with the food which was great for me as I ate most of his food also. When I was done eating, I asked him, "How could you not think that was AMAZING?" He smiled at my innocence and said, "Don't worry son, when we get off this plane and make it to my family's house you will experience real food!"

I don't think either of us realized in that moment how deeply prophetic those words would be. Whenever I asked my Dad why he left the Dominican Republic, he would simply say, "I wanted to give my children an opportunity at a better life". As I sat there quietly second-hand smoking for the next two hours, I thought "If the food is better in his native country maybe we should live there."

As we landed in the capital city of Santo Domingo, the entire plane erupted into a minute long ovation. I waited for my Dad to stop clapping wildly before asking him why everyone was cheering so loudly. He leaned into my ear and said,

"Flying in an airplane is dangerous, so we're celebrating our safe landing."

I looked out my window and saw the ground crew approaching the aircraft with what appeared to be the world's largest staircase. Before long we were deplaning directly onto the runway. The intense New York City humidity I'd grown accustomed to paled in comparison to the sauna-like Caribbean breeze. We walked towards the airport terminal, our vision blurred by the heat haze ascending from the tarmac. As we exited the airport, people were lined up outside like a ticker tape parade awaiting their loved ones when I heard a man yell in our direction "EL GUARDIA!" My father ran towards him and they hugged for what seemed like an eternity. He hadn't seen his brother in almost 15 years since leaving for America and I was beginning to understand why my Dad had so highly anticipated this trip.

"El Guardia", I learned, was my Dad's nickname as he was the only one from his family to have served in the military under Dictator Rafael Trujillo's regime. No one ever called him by his name, only "El Guardia". We drove approximately three hours north to the province of Puerto Plata, my father's birthplace. Along the way we stopped at a food court/rest area in Bonao and got to enjoy a medley of delicious foods. The farther we drove from the airport the more the socioeconomic landscape changed. I was shocked to find that almost everyone was walking around without any shoes and the roads were unpaved. We were escorted to the house where we would be staying. It was a small hut with a tin ceiling and dirt floors. There was no electricity or running water so everyday people went to the nearby river and brought back water for all of their basic needs i.e. drinking, cooking, etc. However nothing could prepare me for my first time in an outhouse. Everyone chuckled at my horror to discover that I'd be relieving myself into a massive hole in the ground inside of a tiny wooden shed.

The next morning we communed for breakfast at my uncle's house which was "just around the corner". Be warned, if a Dominican ever asks you to walk with them just around the corner, you're about to walk at least 2 kilometers. I sat at a table with all my cousins while my parents sat at the adult table and they served us each a bowl of Pops cereal that we had brought from back home.

When they placed my bowl in front of me, I immediately noticed something amiss. First the bowl felt warm to the touch and the "milk" was brown. I was taken aback and called out to my dad saying, "Dad why is the milk brown?" He walked over to me while my cousins giggled at my naiveté and explained that because there was no refrigeration we didn't have milk and that they used a bar of chocolate melted in water to make "milk". What??!!! I'm supposed to eat my cereal devoid of chilled pasteurized milk??!!! This was madness, I thought. With all of the bratty privilege and sense of entitlement that I could muster I said, "Dad....... I need milk to eat my cereal!"

He looked at me with a glare that I have never forgotten. His face was a juxtaposition of indignation and embarrassment. I thought I was about to get the butt whooping of my life. Then suddenly he began to smile. I was confused. "Milk?" he asked. "You need milk?" his sinister grin slowly widening. "No problem Son, I'll get you milk!" He handed my bowl to one of my cousins who had yet to receive their cereal. Then he poured a fresh bowl of cereal and walked outside. I sat there confident that my brazen insolence was about to be rewarded. Several minutes later my dad returned and placed the bowl of cereal in front of me and said, "You wanted milk? There's your milk!", as he walked back to the adult's table. I looked down into my bowl, a beautiful congregation of genetically modified high fructose corn syrup pearls floating in a sea of milk. Without hesitation, I plunged my spoon into the bowl and raised the heaping spoon into my little mouth only to instantly spit it all out. The milk was warm and tasted unlike any milk I had ever had. I didn't understand what was going on? I heard my dad say, "You wanted milk so I went outside and milked a goat for you Son, but not to worry, that's the milk I was raised on...

you'll be fine". The entire room was now laughing at me, my cousins were laughing, the adults were laughing, and as I looked down into my bowl, I could see the somatic cells swirling in the fresh goat milk laughing at me.

This was more than a lesson in humility. I mean, I was humbled for sure but what I really learned in that moment was gratitude. I realized how immensely fortunate and privileged I was to have, as basic amenities of everyday life, that which others would consider luxuries. I immediately began to understand what he meant by, "Giving us a better life."

Six summers later we returned to the Dominican Republic for summer vacation. This trip started differently. First we flew on American Airlines this time. The Salisbury Steak was less impressive than the Hungry Man microwavable dinners we had at home. Also, smoking and second-hand smoking had since been banned on airlines. On this flight, I sat next to my mom who was ecstatic about the new "No Smoking" policy. She told me that we'd be staying in the capital city of Santo Domingo (Yay! No outhouse this time!), and that she needed my help for something that was a secret. This sounded exciting! What possible secret could my mom be concealing, I thought. I asked for more details but she simply told me she'd let me know at the appropriate time.

Back home in New York, I attended a Catholic elementary school. Every year our school handed out cardboard folders to all of the students that contained 40 slots. Each day of Lent we were supposed to put a quarter into a slot and on Easter we'd donate it to the church like a fundraiser of sorts. When I would fill up the cardboard "piggy bank" with quarters and it was time to donate them to the church, my mother would take it from me and tell me we were saving it for something. About two weeks prior to this vacation, my mother gathered all of the folders as well as several little mason jars of spare change she was always collecting. We went to our local Apple Bank to convert the coins into paper bills. Mom was upset when the teller informed us that we needed to first put all of the coins into paper coin holders and write our account number on each one before they could accept them as a deposit. We went back home and I was commissioned with counting and collating the coins. The next day, we returned to the bank to complete the transaction. My mother put the money into an envelope and asked me to write the word "Hospital" on the front.

A few days into our trip, my mother informed me that on this day we'd be carrying out the "secret" she referenced on the plane. First we went to the neighborhood "currency exchange" guy. Every town always had someone who would exchange your American currency into the local currency at a better rate than a "real" currency exchange business. My mom pulled out the small envelope with the word "Hospital" in my handwriting, removed the money and handed it to the man. He counted it, retired to a back room and returned several minutes later. We had only handed the man several bills, yet he returned with what seemed like a huge stack of money. I didn't know that the American dollar was valued differently in other countries. I was fascinated to learn that Dominican "pesos" have different colors depending on their denomination.

She instructed me to distribute the money into envelopes. Some envelopes were to contain $50 pesos, some $100 pesos and a few had $150 pesos. This is why she needed my help. I loved math and everyone in the family always came to me when they had to compute numbers. Then my eldest sister, her husband, my mom and I got into my brother-in-law's jeep and drove off. After about 45 minutes, we arrived in a poverty-stricken neighborhood named "Los Mina".

We walked into a run-down looking building which appeared to be abandoned only to realize THIS was the "Hospital". Back home in New York City, hospitals resembled sophisticated works of modern architecture, not dilapidated structures with flickering lights, cracked walls and the thunderous cacophony of a gas turbine electric generator. It was surreal. We walked down the hall and came to a sign on the wall that read "Sala de Partos" with an arrow pointing in the direction we were heading. Shortly thereafter, we arrived at the maternity ward. I noticed the labor and delivery rooms had no doors so you could peer into each room as you walked by. What I saw was so unfathomable that I just stood there unable to process what I was witnessing.

A large gloomy room painted the color of my dad's Selsun Blue shampoo with six stainless steel tables, three on each side of the room. These tables, outfitted with a single white bed sheet and a tiny pillow, were actually hospital beds. On one side of the room, there were three mothers who had just given birth. They held their newborns wrapped in a small blanket, one mother openly breastfeeding. On the other side of the room were three women in full labor, pushing and breathing to the medical teams' cadence while simultaneously screaming and writhing in pain. As I stood there overwhelmed and confused by this paradox of childbirth, my mother pulled out her envelopes and went into each room handing out envelopes to all the mothers. This was her "Secret".

As she moved from room to room, you could hear the joyful weeping of the mothers who were just realizing the contents of their respective envelopes. When she came out of the last labor room, I noticed she had one envelope left in her hand. We continued walking until we came to a general waiting area. She scanned the room slowly. I wasn't sure what she was looking for and then she walked towards a lady who was sitting with her head down while holding a baby in her arms. She handed the woman the last envelope and turned to walk away. The woman looked into the envelope and jumped up with her baby in tow and ran to my mother. She hugged my mom with her open arm and sobbed violently while yelling, "Hay Dios mio, hay Dios". She was saying, "Oh my God, oh God!" When she finally gathered her composure, she explained to us that she had given birth that morning and because her family was so poor no one could pick them up from the hospital. She said she'd been sitting in the waiting room all morning without eating and was silently begging God for a miracle when we approached her. My mother comforted her and they spoke for a bit before we left.

As we drove back, I couldn't help but be overcome by a suffocating feeling of guilt. I felt guilty for ever being upset with my parents for not buying me all the fancy toys that my friends would brag about at Christmas. I felt guilty for throwing tantrums when I couldn't get McDonald's because "we had food at home". Most of all, I felt guilty for misjudging my mom. You see, every year my dad and I used to dress up in suits and go to Easter mass. My mom never came to church with us. When I'd ask her why she didn't come with us, she would say plainly, "There's many ways to serve God." Before that day, I thought you had to be wealthy to help people in need but I learned that just a few jars of spare change and a loving heart can impact someone's life.

I dedicate this writing to the many people who have influenced and impacted my life. First, my parents Jose Manuel Gonzalez and Venecia Gonzalez, for teaching me the importance of being kind to people and serving others. I'm grateful for your unconditional love and for all the personal sacrifices you both made to make me the man I am today. Thank you Dad for teaching me how to have a strong sense of self-worth without feeling that I'm better than anyone else. Thank you Mom for nurturing my love of cooking and never ever turning your back on me no matter how many mistakes I made. I love you Mom & Dad!

To my daughters, Jasmine Eileen Gonzalez and Alyssa Precious Gonzalez, I could not be more proud of the women you have become. As I've always told you, you have within you the power to shape the life you desire. Always love and respect your mother and always be the author of your own story.

To my son, Jordan Manuel Gonzalez, always cherish and protect your mother and sisters. You possess a strength and spirit of generosity that is as admirable as it is inspiring. I love you and your sisters beyond words.

Heartfelt thanks to my sisters, cousins, friends and family. I carry you all in my heart and my life is enriched by each of you. Thank you to the many mentors and teachers who influenced my ability to think freely and critically. Special thanks to my high school Physics teacher Mr. Messineo for taking the time to teach me how to think and process information. You taught me so much about life and I have never nor could I ever forget you believed in me.

And to my wife, Jeanette, every day I wake up by your side is literally the greatest day of my life. I would not be who I am today without your unflinching love and support. You have stood by me in the best and worst of times and I'm eternally devoted to you. I have never nor would ever love anyone the way I love you. I vow to honor you, protect you and love you all the days of our lives.

Keto MasterChef Jose Gonzalez was born and raised in the Upper Manhattan neighborhood of Washington Heights, New York City. He majored in Culinary Arts & Artisanal Baking and graduated from The French Culinary Institute (later The International Culinary Center) in 1998. After struggling to maintain a healthy weight and lifestyle for over 20 years, he transformed his life by adopting a Ketogenic lifestyle and losing a 100 LBS. Through their company Keto Cooking With Love, he and his wife Jeanette have helped hundreds of people lose thousands of pounds and reverse the onset of chronic diseases with their Meal Prep program; Cooking MasterClasses; and Online Courses and Coaching.

RALPH HENDERSON

I LISTENED TO MY MOTHER

May Lana Connor

Introducing the mother of this humble servant. She simply did for this son that which every mother endeavors to do for their children. She is the most influential because she taught me that every parent owes their child everything and the child owes the parent nothing. She was forever putting me in the best possible circumstances to achieve superior goals. It began with her decision to be my mother rather than the girlfriend and then wife of my father. I remember the day she explained to me why "WE" were leaving my father.

This is the point where she stopped accepting gifts and overtures of love and focused on my education and enrichment. Her proactive actions and finished with a life lesson that would allow me to become a better son and then a better man. She taught me how to have ambition and achieve great heights. She held me accountable for every circumstance I would find myself. She was principal in every way and the best part of our relationship that I was certain that she was the person on earth least trying to hurt me. As a result, she taught me patience and listening skills. She explained that you have to listen to know what you need to take forward from the moment. She led by example by barely graduating from high school and then attending community college and graduating from New York University with a degree in education.

She put her life on the back burner by all indications so it was almost a mandate that I go at least as far as she did educationally. She supported everything ambition that I had and she did not always understand the goals I made for myself but she was excellent at making support of those goals a directive for the both of us. Her personality was brusque and her communication style was extremely direct. She instructed me to look people in the eye and not to blink, literally or virtually; she instructed me to be a man in all circumstances and know that I had a duty to humanity to try and leave this world a little better than I found it. She explained that I was the best and the brightest and I had a nobility that required me to "lift all boats". She made me eligible to approach and be accepted by the next person that was most influential.

Patricia Louise Lindsay

I met Pat as the result of a chance encounter in which I met a high school classmate of hers. I picked his name at random because he was from Philly; I figured he was probably a cool frosh. I grew up with her in college and then as a young adult. While she was overachieving, I was simply bouncing from one impulse to another. As we aged she began to ask more of me as a man and a potential companion. I began to listen to her as she guided me through a vast array of new experiences and ambitions. She implanted in me a need to seek and do more. She allowed me the space to discover myself in the context of adulthood and all that encompasses; professional development as well as fatherhood and community fellowship.

She married me and put a home in place and then family with the addition of my son Quincy. At this point she extracted from me a level of development that I had not realized I had available. She taught and assisted me in every aspect of my growth as a man; for selfish reasons of course. She explained that I would not be able to be an also ran when there was so much that was great inside me. She with a gentle but firm hand guided me to the top of an extremely competitive profession in engineering and then Information Technology consulting. She gave me the greatest gift a man can receive from any influential personality; she explained that I am not just one thing, I am many things. She gave me the impetus to be all that I could and wanted. She inspired and encouraged me to remember engineering school where I was taking multiple technical classes and multiple math course every semester. She reminded me of the simple power of my thoughts and ambitions.

These are powers she martialed in me with the simple turns of phrases and the reminder that there was nothing but faith in me to care for the family. She inspired me by becoming something she never seem to be interested in; becoming a fulltime mom. Even though she missed her professional endeavors she became an amazing mom. She learned about her challenges at least as much as I about mine. She continues to inspire me today because she has been stricken with Alzheimer's disease and faces it with nothing but strength and dignity. She is aware of her condition and she has never asked "why me". I am only hoping to be a fraction of the person that she is going forward.

Ralph Edward Henderson Jr. Mine is the simplest of stories. It can be summed up by declaring here that I listened to my mother. She instructed me and I followed her instructions simply because she was never going to hurt me. That being said, it all started in a head start in Harlem, NY. I went to a school in Harlem for two years and then moved to a Montessori school for two years directed by graduate students at Columbia University. The school closed and then off to Catholic School for a year, then a public school in Riverdale, NY for a year. Junior high school for two years in Riverdale, NY and off to The Bronx High School of Science. Graduating from Bronx Science I attended Rensselaer Polytechnic Institute where I earned a degree in Nuclear Engineering.

I went to work at an engineer architectural firm Combustion Engineering, bought by ASEA Brown Boveri. Got an opportunity to be employed at the largest nuclear utility in the world in Arizona Public Service. From there I decided to change directions and became an I.T. consultant. Became a very competent and sought after consultant and in that space Pat was stricken with Alzheimer's and I stopped working to take care of her. I looked around for a new profession, tried some things and settled on life insurance. This was a natural fit because I had used life insurance in my personal finances and estate planning. I also became the CFO of The Matthews Broadcast, aka The Matthews Business Network. At this point the story is still being written.

RHONDA LEONARD-HORWITH

Through war with honor
Through adversity with courage
Thought out with each other
~Tuskegee Airmen

MY FATHER AND GRANDFATHER

Understanding the immense influence that my father, Lt. Col. Harlan Q. Leonard Jr. had on my personality, actions, and career is to first understand his father, Harlan Q. Leonard Sr. Born in 1905 in Kansas City, Missouri, Harlan Sr. quickly developed a love of fine clothes, fine barbeque, good music, and an appreciation for discipline and saving money.

By 17, he became a professional musician and joined the Benni Moten orchestra. He went on to play with the Kansas City Skyrockets before forming his own band, "Harlan Leonard and His Rockets." The band quickly became a leading band in the Kansas City area, toured nationally, and was instrumental in carving out the "Kansas City Jazz Era." Charlie Parker, who later developed the "bebop" style, played with the band for five weeks but was fired by Harlan Leonard for disciplinary issues. The discipline, saving, love of the big band sound, and my grandfather's finely tuned skills as a barbeque master were directly inherited by my father and passed on to me.

I often listen to my grandfather's old recordings as they are available on the internet. I absolutely love to immerse myself in the sounds of the Big Band Era. Whenever I would visit my grandfather, he would put on a record on the record player, bring out a roll of quarters, have me sit in his lap, count the quarters, and tell him how many I was going to save. My father always made us save 10% of all the money we earned I earned or was given as a gift. Harlan Q. Leonard Jr. proudly gave me a little budget book with columns and lines. I had to map out my weekly expenditures so I could tell him where every cent of my allowance and babysitting money was going. When it was time to get my first car, he loaned me the money and charged me less interest than the dealer. His philosophy was to keep the money circulating in the family. My grandfather did the same with his band members. When they would spend all their money, he would lend it to them at a low interest. It is no wonder that I have developed a love of teaching budgeting and how money works!

My dad, like my grandfather, was the barbeque king in the family. My grandfather would order his steaks from Kansas City and only cook on a particular kind of grill. I definitely inherited that skill set. To this day, I am the "Queen Bee of the BBQ" with my own unique tools, a smoker, and a Santa Maria grill. My father, also a fine musician (saxophone), developed a love for flying that overpowered his love of music. At the age of 19, he answered the call for black pilots and headed south to train at Tuskegee Institute. He said the "wash out rate" at Tuskegee was 80%! The white instructors did everything they could to try and prove black men could not be pilots. They trained in substandard planes discarded by their white counterparts. He lost many classmates as planes stopped working, falling from the sky. My father's sayings: "never give up, no matter how difficult, no matter how bad you feel", "don't compare yourself to others", and "always complete the mission" are the foundation that keep me going in my business and life today.

"Complete the mission" he did. The discipline gleaned from his father directly lent itself to the discipline needed to fly against seemingly unbeatable odds. As a result, Harlan Q. Leonard Jr. became one of the Original Tuskegee Airmen. He flew 9 different aircraft types, won top flying honors, earned his Master's Degree in Physics, taught Math for the United States

Air Force, worked for the National Security Agency, and retired as a Lieutenant Colonel. To this day, I remain in awe of my dad and all his accomplishments. I wanted nothing more than to please him, which led me to the college and career paths I chose. I loved science, numbers and the arts.

My father had one continual challenge he would place before my sisters and me: to be better than he was when we got to be the age he was. Oh, how I loved a challenge! He loved giving them to us to make us perform at the highest level. So that challenge was constantly ringing in my ears. He got one college degree, I got two with a minor in theater arts. He got a Master's, I got a Master's. I became the first in my family to take it to the next level by earning my Juris Doctorate. He worked as an electrical engineer, I worked as a mathematician for the Navy. He loved his Engineering magazine; I published an article in the International Electronic Engineering Magazine. I answered his every challenge.

When my mother taught my sisters and me to sew, my dad perfected our skills. Each time we completed an article of clothing, he would lay it out. It had to pass inspection. He would lay a ruler next to the seams; we had to take it out if the stitching was crooked As a result, my sisters and I became professional seamstresses and earned good money designing and sewing for people during our college years. My dad always took the time to listen to both sides of the story before making a decision. He would sit us down and talk it out if we had an issue. He taught us respect for people's property, to return things in better shape than when we received them. He taught us respect for mother earth and all her creatures. He raised us in the Audubon society. He taught us to experience everything life had to offer. We visited all the museums, historical sites, national parks camped all over the southwest, including but not limited to the Shenandoah's and Canada. He enrolled us in piano and put us in every sports lesson available. He even took us to visit different churches so we could make an informed decision as to which one we wanted to attend. There was no debate on the subject of college: we were expected to go, and we all did. Above all, he taught us to always respect and protect the family.

Daddy, you are the steadfast pillar in my life with your kind word, wisdom, blunt but constructive criticism, kindness, gentleness, no hesitation to crack the whip when necessary, or laugh with me and cry with me. You taught me the value of family, religion, nature, saving, sharing, humbleness and created an indestructible bond. These principles are the glue that keeps me together. You poured life and belief into me. I love being your little girl. For you, I have endless gratitude.

My Mom

My mother, Bertha "Bunny" Leonard, taught me how to cook, stretch a dollar, enlarge my dreams, sew and be creative. She wanted me to have limitless income streams, always do what is right even when no one is looking, and always be home before the streetlights came on. My mom was the polar opposite of my dad. My dad was technical and analytical, whereas my mother was a social and creative butterfly paying much attention to detail. Bunny made friends everywhere she went.

Bertha gave the best birthday parties ever! I will never forget my seventh birthday party. I was born on George Washington's birthday; she placed a tumbleweed branch in the middle of the table and tied dozens of cherries to the branches to make it look like a cherry tree. I never forgot the amazement on my face and the others when they saw that cherry tree. As a direct result, I am known throughout the entire family for throwing the best parties, holidays included! One Easter, when my daughter was asleep, I drew little tiny paw prints on her cheek and her pillow and told her the Easter bunny had been on her bed and touched her face. She didn't wash her face for a week! I have also enjoyed giving my family & friends the same pleasure my mother afforded me on my special day.

My mother grew up between Philadelphia and New York. She hung out with her cousins, and they were not to be tampered with. If you messed with one of them, you messed with all of them. One day, we looked in her trunk and found black leather boots, pants, and a jacket. I said: "Mama, were you a gangster?" She said: "No, baby, I was just part of the social club." So, of course, I envisioned my mom as part of a motorcycle gang from that point on. I think my mom's upbringing was part of why she ruled with an iron fist. My mother poured everything she had, body and soul, into her kids, but I knew that if I crossed her, talked back, questioned her authority, or rolled my eyes, there would be Hell to pay. She would go outdoors, find a willow branch, strip the leaves, be back in the house, and wrap it around my leg before lightning struck. Needless to say, we rarely crossed my mom and were on the porch before the streetlights came on.

Lord could Bunny cook! I learned barbecuing from my dad and the fine art of cooking from my mom! She would say, "The way to a man's heart is through his stomach" and "Don't waste, we eat everything but the oink!" From scratch, she could make anything: prize-winning gumbo, jambalaya, cakes, cookies, cornbread, yeast rolls, bread, lemonade, icing, silky gravy, and the smoothest hand-churned ice cream, to mention a few. I would be in awe watching her cook. She had lots of recipe books but never seemed to use them. I would say: "How much do you put in?" She would say: "Just a dash or just a skosh or just a smidgen." I'd ask: "What is a smidgen" She would say: "It's smaller than a dash." I made sure I learned how to cook everything from my mom. When my kids ask me how much to put in, I find myself saying the same thing: "Just a skosh."

Mom was always crafty; she sewed, did upholstery & ceramics. My father would give her an allowance; she always skimmed some off the top to buy a little something for us and stashed the rest in different places around the house. I remember when I was pregnant, my mom said: "Girl, you can't sit up at that house and be pregnant! You need to get out there and make some money in case something happens". So we sold things together at the craft fair. I made jewelry, she sold ceramics. She always had to have different ways to make money. She's the reason I was in so many different marketing businesses, always trying to hustle that extra dollar. Thank you, mom! You'd be proud of my business today!

Bunny was a stickler for chores. We always had a chores chart to earn our allowance. She would have us up at the crack of dawn to do our tasks. We were not allowed to sleep in. "Get your chores done so you'll feel good about yourself, then you can go back to sleep." I always wondered how I was possibly supposed to go back to sleep after two hours of cleaning. To this day, I do my best work early in the morning.   She taught us how to separate, wash, fold and iron our clothes and cook the basics before we got out of elementary school, and I did the same for my kids. My mom always taught me to do the job right, and just like my dad said, "Always do a little bit extra," (I earned 26 Girl Scout badges in one year)!

One of the biggest influences my mother had on me was the love of family. We were lucky enough to be stationed on the East Coast because her family was in Philadelphia and New York. Every Thanksgiving and New Year, we went to Philadelphia for the big family dinner and the New Year's Eve party. I remember the aroma's coming through the house as we walked into the brownstone. There was always lots of food. I thought they were feeding an army. Now my husband says the same to me: "So much food. Are we feeding an army?"

THE "FAB 5"

A total shift, an entirely new era, was ushered into my life, with my most outstanding achievement, my "Fab 5"... Tahir, Amirah, Amber, Shawn, and Niko. They are my heart and soul, my sparkling jewels. They taught me life lessons I did not know I needed to learn!   I love you all to the moon and back. You are my treasures. They taught me to love without limits and that everyone has gifts locked inside of them, waiting to be discovered. They have taught me that each new day is a gift.

They try my patience, test my abilities, and push my creativity to the limit. The "Fab 5" became the "Magnificent 7" with the addition of spouses David and Jennifer and then became the "Glorious 8" with the birth of my three precious grandchildren, Sophia, Miles, and Julius. They keep me pumped, fired up, and super excited. So, thank you forever for just being you. I will always be here for you loving you unconditionally. To this day, family is number one in my life.

***

To those who opened the door of the possibility of possibilities: It is with great pleasure that I submit this letter of love, appreciation, and gratitude to those from days gone by whose spirits live on, from those that continue to highlight the present and to pay respect to those yet to come. I hope you will truly feel the appreciation and love I have for you.

I must initially pay homage, and awe-inspiring admiration for those forced here on slave ships and the natives on the reservations who gave them refuge. Your suffering and cries for freedom are not forgotten and echo in my soul. I hear you, I see you, and I feel you, what you have to say matters. My backbone is your pure stone-cold courage, true grit, fortitude, endurance, and persistence. You have encouraged me to keep up the fight, never quit.

My deepest gratitude, appreciation, and admiration for the man I met when I was tackling the difficult task of being a single parent of two while attending USC Law School. My deepest gratitude to the man who stepped up to the plate when I needed it most, came to the rescue, and assisted me with my rambunctious 3 and 6-year-olds, who married me and made three more sparkling additions to the family, producing the "Fab 5". My undying gratitude to Jeff, the love of my life. Even with rough patches, even when the road gets rocky, through sorrow, joy, sickness, and loss of loved ones. We mesh learning tolerance and expanding the meaning of love.

To my twin sisters Myrna and Karla and their children Dagan, Josh, Alana, and her beautiful twin babies, Ilia, with her babies Aurelius, Eloisa, Andrew, and the respective girlfriends and spouses. I am indebted to you for your shoulders to lean on when we all experienced the difficulties of surviving as single mothers.

Genuine appreciation to my Auntie Jo - the high fashion designer, free-spirited entrepreneur who taught me to be in control of my own time, money, and magic. Genuine appreciation goes to my grandmother Bernice Leonard and my great-grandmother Inez Pennington, who demonstrated and taught me perfection in the kitchen and serving. To cousin Eddie Mae, Godmother Nani, cousins Beverly, Sidney, Yvonne and Sparky, Aunt Flo, and bigger than life, cousin William "WH" Harper, who at six foot, four inches, always commands respect. You all steeped me in family spirit, kept me laughing, created lifelong memories. Even though small, our maternal family is mighty!

I have been showered with blessings, beliefs, confidence, patience, understanding, and discipline, thoughtful and kind words. I have been taught to see the good in others and am prepared to leave this world better than I found it. I dream big and teach others to do the same. I'm blessed; each day is a gift to be opened and enjoyed. The universe has my back, and all of you have and continue to be part of that universe.

Imani Nia Haba Na Haba Lala Salama, (With Faith and focus, little by little, your cup will be filled, sweet dreams)

With love,

Rhonda, Mom, TuTu

Rhonda Leonard-Horwith was born at Temple University Hospital in Philadelphia, Pennsylvania, to Lt. Col. Harlan Q. Leonard Jr, retired, an Original Tuskegee Airmen, Air Force pilot, engineer, and Bertha Leonard. She grew up moving across the United States and earned a Bachelor of Arts degree in Mathematics and one of the original first two Bachelor of Arts degrees awarded in Black Studies with a minor in Theater Arts.

Mrs. Leonard-Horwith went on to work as one of the first three black women scientists hired by the US Naval Undersea Research

& Development Center in Pasadena, California. Her work there resulted in a publication in an International Electronic Engineering Journal. She earned her MBA from the University of Michigan. She then worked as an industrial engineer for one year at Kaiser Steel and six years in the healthcare planning arena for Inland County Health Systems Agency. After earning her Juris Doctor degree at the University of Southern California, she worked 33 years for the L.A. County Public Defender as a trial attorney. Finally, in 2016 she returned to the financial education arena.

ANTHONY MARIA "A.M." NOEL

WHEN YOU CONCIEVE AND BELIEVE, THE PATH OPENS UP FOR YOU

Lourdes Mary Elizabeth

My mother was one of 13 children when the country was called Malaya. The tradition is marriage was arranged by the elders of the respective families. As she and her sisters approached marriageable age, they were betrothed to men selected by the family or matchmakers. This was the time when all marriages were arranged. Her sister was proposed to by my father but the moment my father saw my mom, he knew she was the one he wanted to marry and to the fiery consternation of the rest of the family, they fell in love and got married. The guts she had to buck the system and trounce age-old norms was the first and most inspiring thing about my mother, Lourdes Mary Elizabeth. The couple went on to have several children. I was ninth of their batch of 10 children (the child Catherine died after 3 days), scores of grand children and many great grand children. All told, there were about 122 direct descendants of that union between Lourdes Mary and my father Anthony Samy - a lasting legacy.

Through all the challenges of World War 1 after Dad came home just a few days before my eldest sister, Mary Theresa's wedding, an arson by a jealous relative burned part of our house and left us in extreme poverty, she kept her children safe and the family together, getting all of them married off successfully. I don't think I had ever seen my mother agitated. Her deep faith in God and love for her family kept her in a perpetual state of serenity.

My father presented her with a different kind of challenge, as difficult as all the others. During the Second World War,

Dr. Subha Chandra Bose, an army officer from India came to Malaya to recruit young men to the war to fight for India. My father immediately said yes to the Indian army and approached my mom and asked if she had any valuables she could donate to the cause. The only thing she had of worth was her wedding gold chain. She immediately took it off and gave it to him and he went to the war. Mum joined under the women's wing under Janasrani and sewed uniforms for the soldiers. At this time, her oldest son was only 12 and she took him off school because he was the only one who could earn money. He sold scrap iron and the money he earned was used to buy food for the four children. For 4 years there was no salary, no electricity, no proper water system and she had to think of creative ways to feed the 4 children, never in the process losing her calm. My sisters learnt how to grow tapioca. That was the staple food during the war.

My mother woke up at four each morning, cooked breakfast for my father, then the children. My father returned home at 6'oclock each evening, had dinner that she had prepared and then left each night to work as a negotiator for the railway union. As the number of children grew, she had to cook for nine children making sure that we had the adequate sustenance to keep us alert in school.

In 1963 she took 4 of us to India for our education and spent five years in India. Because of difficulties with language and the climate, she fell sick and put my brother Mogan Chandra Dass in boarding school in India and went back to Malaysia. She went to mass every day and said the rosary every single day before going to bed at 10 PM or later.

My mother was the queen of one-liner wisdom that she instilled in us so deeply that I still remember them. Her favorite sayings to all of us were:

- "Tell the truth and shame the Devil"
- "A stitch in time saves nine"
- "With God anything is possible"
- "Don't put off until tomorrow what you could do today"

- "Keep away from people who do not make you feel good"
- "Don't pour hot water on your own foot"
- "Do unto others what you want done to you"
- "Live within your means"
- "Measure many times and cut only once"

SAVRIMUTHU ANTHONY SAMY

The story begins with this young kid in a tiny village in India who loved to play. The head student was sent to find this kid. The kid noticed the head student that yelled his name was Savrimuthu Anthony Samy. On hearing his name this kid went into the village lake, would jump into the lake, hold his breath as long as he could and slowly peek out of the lake to make sure no one was there, especially the head student. He would run into paddy fields and play with the goats and ride on top of the cow like a horse. Seeing the poverty in the village, when he was seven years old, his family travelled on a ship for 10 days and moved to Malaysia. This kid is none other than my father.

When he first came to Malaya someone brought a stool to sit on. He climbed on the stool and squatted and everyone laughed. He could not understand why. He had never seen stools in his life because people squatted on the floor in India. The only time he went to school was to give speeches later in life.

His Accomplishments:

- Love and marriage to my mom when most marriages were arranged.
- Married for 67 years.
- Had 10 children.
- Several grandchildren and great grands.
- Enrolled in the Indian National Army.
- Fought in the Second World War.
- United the Indian community together.
- A founding member of the Malaysian Indian Congress.

- Was instrumental in gaining Independence for Malaysia.
- Met the first Prime Minister of Malaysia.
- Won several awards for various leadership roles.
- Given the title PPN from the king of Malaysia.
- Organized the biggest strike in Malaysia and moved from daily wages to monthly wages,

What I learned from him:

- Connect with as many people as I can in life.
- Be grateful.
- Deal with what is given to you.
- Be brave, take risk.
- Travel the world.
- Never stop working.
- Go the extra mile.

MARY THERESA

One of the biggest inspirations of my life is my sister Mary Theresa. Her eldest son, Dr. Charles Arokiasamy is also very important to me, almost an extension of her influence. Being almost of the same age, Charles was 8 months older than I, we grew up together. From childhood, Charles has been a mentor up to this very day.

Mary Theresa was the oldest of my nine siblings and in a real sense my second mother. I had always called her Big Mummy, picking up from Charles and his siblings, who called her Mummy. She had a heart of gold. She treated me as one of her own. She borrowed money and bought me and Charles our first notebook. I was probably 5 years old. She taught us how to write the letters of the alphabet and we spent the entire day writing the alphabet multiple times till I finished the entire notebook. I saw my very first television set in her house. She bought an old car, hired a driver, went to the rubber estates and taught the uneducated people how to plan family and life.

No matter what time of the day, anyone who came to her household could count on being served delicious food. I used to bring all kinds of strangers and she would never complain and always had an excellent meal, even though her family was poor. That meant, of course, she often went without food herself. Everyone she met was special and she treated everyone the same as royalty. Big Mummy was indefatigable, rising at 4 or 5 in the morning, to do the massive amount of laundry of all her siblings and their and her children, by hand. Even the day after she delivered one of her children, she was back at work the very next day. Of course, when the clothes were dried on clotheslines in the Malaysian sun, she had to collect them and iron them in the afternoon using a metal iron with red hot coals in its base. Cleanliness was important to her being almost obsessive. She taught us cleanliness and kept everything arranged and clean. Anything that she started, she would not stop until it was complete and done to the best of her ability. It was rare to see her not doing something.

Tireless, Big Mummy would never stop teaching herself new things all the time. She learnt Japanese during the Japanese occupation during World War II. She taught herself Punjabi and Hindi when she had Punjabi neighbors. She taught herself knitting and made scarfs and baby socks for women in the family who recently had children. She ALWAYS had other children living in her house caring for them when their family had difficulties. Many of my nephews and nieces were raised by her, all calling her Big Mummy. When everyone else in the community was cooking their ethnic treats for religious festivals like Christmas, Chinese New Year or Hari Raya (for Muslims), she taught herself western baking and taught the neighborhood to bake cakes and cookies. Sometimes people would place orders with her for cakes and cookies, even up to 5000 Pineapple Jam Tarts that she would bake and deliver in a day or two. This was supplemental income for her to feed her family. Because she often had neighbors in her house learning how to bake, her house almost always had the smell of something baking. As baking technology evolved, she taught herself to use the latest ovens. The first cakes she baked were in a pan that needed fire underneath and hot coals on top, her own makeshift oven. All of the children helped with mixing the dough or beating egg whites.

Big Mummy taught me how to treat everyone with full respect and to love even people that harm us. Her principle was that everyone should look and be the best. I can't recall her saying no to anyone. I remember her giving away her own sons' best clothes to me because they looked better on me. She used to tell us to always be early to everything in life and made sure we loved everyone.

***

This section of the book is dedicated to roughly 70,000 generations that it took to make who I am today and the rest of my life on this planet. I am also dedicated to my daughter Saraswati Noel, son Jeevan Noel, and every single person that will be coming to this planet. In short, every living object yet to come.

Most important of all to the person who is and will be reading this after I have left this planet:

> ***REMEMBER YOU ARE UNIQUE AND
> SPECIAL. YOU ARE THE ONE THE FUTURE
> GENERATIONS ARE WAITING FOR. ANYONE
> CAN SAVE ANYONE, ANYTIME. WHEN YOU
> CONCEIVE AND BELIEVE, THE PATH OPENS UP
> FOR YOU... THE ONE READING THIS NOW.***

Anthony Maria "A.M." Noel was born in 1953, the ninth child of a family of 10 and grew up in Malaysia, except for high school in India. His passion was to make a difference. He ended up in the seminary studying for the Catholic priesthood. He later realized that his passion was to help people directly, and joined the ICA, spending 15 years working with that disadvantaged people in about 20 different countries on 5 continents. He now resides in

Washington, DC with his wife. Noel has two children, a daughter, Saraswati Noel, who is finishing her Doctoral studies in Math Education in Washington State, and a son, Jeevan Noel, who is a triathlete.

DR. RENEE TENGELLA

INTEGRITY, RESPONSIBILITY AND POSITIVE HABITS

Mama's Love: Her Actions Spoke Louder Than Her Words

My mother, whom I lovingly called Ma, significantly impacted my life, and how she influenced me is not straightforward as one might think, for the lessons are hidden in the twists and turns of my life story. My mother was born in 1936, and she was the eldest of eight children. Ma was born in one of the few historic black towns in Maryland called Turner Station, and in 1958, she married her high school sweetheart, my daddy. This tumultuous union brought four children into the world and I am the youngest girl, or the middle child, who was born on July 1st, my mother's birthday.

Being that we both shared the same birthday, her priorities as a mother taught me so much about family such as respect, sacrifice, responsibility and love. Mama shared her birthday with me until she died and she always made me feel special on our big day. It was only when I got older, that I began to see the uniqueness about being born on my mother's birthday. There are many questions that continue to be unanswered like why didn't I have a separate celebration, and why didn't I have my own birthday cake? But it's ok, because what matters most is that I am forever connected to her. My mom passed in 2014, but July 1st continues to be the day I acknowledge and celebrate with her, because her life has taught me much about honoring, connecting and respecting my elders and ancestors.

RESPONSIBILITY

I am the middle child, and so I was wedged between my eldest sister, my oldest brother, and my youngest sibling, who had a vision disability. Although I was positioned third in the family, I was treated like I was the eldest by being given household chores at an early age, as well as helping to take care of my younger siblings. For some reason, it seemed that there was much more expected of me than from my other siblings.

Often, I was expected to do the tasks that my mother was too tired to do and these were tasks that were not delegated to my eldest brother, who received all of the special privileges, nor to my younger brother who was visually impaired and definitely not my older sister who was either living with my grandmother, attending school or working. Through her actions and sacrifices, my mother taught me that it was not about me, but, my responsibility was to the family.

LOVE LESSONS

I am ashamed to say this, but my mother really never affectionately said to me; *"I love you."* I mean, maybe she did when I was much too young to remember, but as I came of age, she just didn't express her love verbally. For many years, I felt unloved and looked for love in all the wrong places, and I made many unfortunate decisions based on external validation.

Deep in my heart, I longed for her to say, to mutter, and to whisper to me: "I love you daughter." Although she never did, I learned to let it go, and later I developed compassion for her life and upbringing. Over time, I had accepted the fact that my mother did the best she could, and she only mirrored how her mother, my grandmother, and my grandfather loved her.

I've also learned that saying the words; *"I love you"* alone is not a complete statement. This has also taught me that the old proverb is true, "actions speak louder than words." Not hearing those words from my mother have propelled me to embrace self-love, and it has also convinced me to break the generational cycle of not expressing love to my children. I have learned from her mistakes and without hesitation, I now say to my children out loud that "I love you!" and with action, I demonstrate my love for them in many ways.

FAMILY

Additionally, the importance of family was something that my mother passed down to me and my siblings, and her struggle to keep the family together still resonates with us today. She was the oldest in a family of seven siblings and she was all about family gatherings, family dinners, playing cards and games. Ma demonstrated her love by her sacrifices she made for her children and the late night shifts she worked for us, trying to maintain a family, so she could send us off to school in the morning.

The financial sacrifices my mother made during the strain in my parents' marriage were also demonstrated. As we continue to take trips together, celebrate each other and gather for family reunions, dinner, cards or sports on occasion, I want to say thank you Ma for your life and your legacy. To my children, much love to each of you.

My paternal grandmother was the matriarch of the family, a churchgoing Christian woman, with a strong faith and belief in God. Not very verbose or loud, but when she spoke,

My grandmother, Margaret, who l lovingly called Grandma influenced me as a child and shaped me into the person that I am today, because her life and legacy continues to influence me in so you heard her loud and clear. My grandmother was born in Cumberland County, Virginia in 1914, and at the age of eighteen, she was married and when she turned twenty-two, she had moved north to Baltimore.

By the time I was born, I do not believe my mother and father was ready for me to come into this world. Now that I think about it, I realized that I was probably that "oops" child. I wasn't an outright mistake, however, I was not planned either. I say that because my sister and brother were already here, one being five and the other one was six. In retrospect, it seemed that there were things, (nurturing, love, care, etc.) in my child-hood that were just missing.

That is where the Creator tapped my grandmother on the shoulder asking her to step in, look out for me and fill in the gap. My grandmother provided me with the nurturing, security and love that I missed from my parents. She did not adopt me, although I wished she had, but we visited her often. With every visit we had, it was me that she often encouraged and motivated me.

My grandmother was the one person in my life who had set aside time just for me. Seemingly, my mother was busy work-ing and my father was around but not living with us. My sib-lings being years older than me, were busy with school, friends etc. While everyone was busy,

Grandmother was there to take care of me, to bring posi-tivity and joy into my life. Just her mere presence soothed and eased all that I longed for, and that was to be loved.

My Grandma's memories of being a strong family support-er continues now even as an adult. Moving from place to place caused turmoil in our family, so we sought refuge in grand-mother's house, making it the go-to place for stability and a place called home. Even though my family moved around a lot, the doors to her home were always opened to us, which pro-vided a consistent place of connection to my family but most importantly, it kept the family connected to our father.

When I was born, in 1964, my paternal grandmother was already an elder in her 50's. She was established in the com-munity, married twice, and a homeowner. Her love for family influenced me because she was symbolic of the love and the attention that I needed so much in my life. I can never ever re-member a time that she spoke to me harshly or treated me with anything except love.

Grandma's house was the place where our family would gather on special occasions and holidays and it was the place where we would travel from the city on the bus just so we could connect with her and my father. At Grandma's small two bedroom house in Turner Station, Maryland, we would gather around the makeshift kitchen table in the living room to have a meal where grace was said and everyone ate at the same time. My grandmother was also the one who passed down to us the tradition of family reunion, in her hometown, Cumberland County, VA. She planned and made sure that we connected with her side of the family.

Grandma taught me the true meaning of confidence and how to believe in myself. She also taught me how to have a positive outlook on life and possess the strength to face this world and all of its problems.

My grandmother's life provided me with love, security, stability, family connection, and confidence that I truly needed as a child and even now as an adult.

My big sister, Roz, influenced me by allowing me to live and learn in her shadow. I am now just realizing how much of an influence she has had on my life. She is my only big sister who is six years older than me. From when I was born, I watched Roz all of my life and have learned so much from her about living in this world as a positive little Black girl. Even today and I don't know if she even knows it, my big sister continues to teach and model for me daily about integrity, responsibility, and other positive habits. It seems like many elders in our family has passed away from smoking cigarettes or a pipe. Roz, like myself was exposed to smoking, however, she never decided to develop a smoking habit, and as of this day, she nor I smoke.

My sister is not one to argue and because of her peaceful temperament, we really never had a fight. I mean we've had a few disagreements, but none that lasted very long. We disagreed one time in the 70's when she took my boyfriend, when I was a kid around six-years old.

He was totally not my age, and not my boyfriend either, but I was mad, yet we had no beef, but I just never let her forget it.

Another thing about my sister is that she knows how to keeps a secret, and just like a fortress, she won't tell your secret. She is also a person of her word, which is also a personality trait of mines too.

I used to get mad at her when I was the last to find out something in the family, but I couldn't be mad too long because she was just keeping her word, by keeping it a secret. She was not one for talking about people, their business or telling their secrets. She was never a gossiper, and neither am I.

My sister was never a fighter, and she never had a physical fight in school or the community. Now that I think about it, I don't recall her ever being in trouble, in a fight or a disagreement with anyone, and she didn't hang with people who brought nonsense either. She chose her friends wisely, and through her example, she taught me how to do the same.

***

I dedicate this book to Frances and Willie Allen, my parents, who without their union, I would not be here. Without their lives and their union, I would cease to exist, and none of the things in my life would I have become.

I also dedicate this book to my only daughter, my eldest, Renata, who continues to amaze me and make me proud. May you continue to shine as a bright reflection of your mother (me). Keep being an amazing outstanding woman and I thank you for being my first child; the one who helped me to become the mother that I am today--for being the sensible child, and now the adult. I am proud of who you have become..

To my twin sons, Omaje and Nkosi, you both are my son-shine, and I am proud of who you both are growing up to become, therefore, I celebrate your strength, intelligence and your respectability as young men. As my twin boys, your individuality and uniqueness continues to make me proud, now and in the future.

To my grandson-Kyrie, you are a blessing to this family, because you bring us so much, joy and happiness. You are my *"GrandSun,"* so continue to shine.

To my husband Koli, my rock, my protector, my love, and my friend. Your growth and willingness to be your best continues to amaze me every day, and for that, our lives together never ends.

To my one sister, my many brothers, aunts, uncles, and cousins, without you I would not be. May this book inspire you!

Love You So Much …Always, Mom, Nana. Renee

Dr. Renee Tengella is a career educator, author, writer, speaker, mother, daughter, sister and wife. She was born as the youngest girl in a family of four children, on the East Coast of the United States. Dr. Tengella is a passionate and dedicated community member who gives back to youth and families through being an educator for the last 22 years. Dr. Tengella's teaching experience, community leadership and commitment to community wellness expands more than three decades. She currently serves as director of Peaceful Warriors, a non-profit organization promoting the importance of community wellness especially for teachers, students and families. She believes that to do the work of teaching, or any profession, one must be healthy, take care and prioritize themselves first in order to continue the work. Dr. Tengella's passions and interest include travel, bike riding, exercise, yoga, mindfulness, and meditation.

MICHELLE WALKER-DAVIS

THE WOMEN OF POWER AND MEN OF VALOR THAT SHAPED MY REALITY

My amazing upbringing by a Woman of Power and Man of Valor gave me a global perspective of humanity, humility, and legacy! Who influenced my growth and development as a woman of power, wife, mother, entrepreneur, philanthropist, global leader, change agent, and to be unstoppable? There have been many but my top three are, my Mother, Father, and the Davis 6. To understand me better is to know my upbringing and family impact.

MY BIGGEST CHEERLEADERS

I was the first in my family to graduate from college and go on to earn dual master's degrees from Syracuse University, whereas my older siblings would start and not finish. Dennis chose a rewarding career in the Army, Maureen got married, and Lamont chose business ownership. My parents would be there for me every step, every hurdle, to cheer me on. As a result, our whole extended family became Syracuse Orangemen. My parents were so proud, that when they asked me what I wanted for a graduation present I said a brand-new BMW and that's what I got!

It was delivered on a Friday, and I drove it home from Syracuse stripping gears along the way as my first job out of college would begin on Monday in Philadelphia. Let's just say, that car posed a problem for me and my co-workers as I did not know a BMW stood for a Black Man's Wish!

I could do ALL things with these two dynamos, my biggest cheerleaders pushing, praying, and believing in ME! My parents supported higher education and was very proud of the 20 plus degrees held by their legacies. They made it a priority to attend every graduation, no matter the distance or health issues. Through this union, they produced six children, thirteen grandchildren, and four great-grands, and a host of beloved nieces and nephews. My parents were soul mates and would go on to celebrate 67 years of marriage and leave this earth one right after the other, together, forever. As a military brat, yes I was spoiled but not spoiled rotten!

MARY ELIZABETH FULMORE WALKER, WOMAN OF POWER, GRACE, & STYLE

Mary Elizabeth Fulmore Walker was a powerful woman with grace, style, amazing strength, and beauty. This 90-lb woman, the oldest of five daughters, Pearlie, Shirley, Kay and Arnetha known as the "Fulmore Girls" would rise to the ranks of family matriarch when her mother died at an early age. Mom was the "rock" and "pillar of strength" to the family. Everything I learned about womanhood, self-determination, being relentless, bold and fearless, I learned from this small in stature yet iconic in status, woman. Mom always said, "One mother could take care of 10 children but 10 children could not take care of one mother. Mom preached truth! Her other mantra was "Mommas baby, daddy's maybe" was to serve as a reminder of no disputing whose responsibility it was for child bearing, childrearing, and lifelong sacrifice. All her colloquialisms were to transcend life.

My Mother was born to the late Jesse and Priscilla Fulmore on October 18, 1935, in Williamsburg, SC. Her father, a military man, moved to Burlington City, NJ where he later owned Fulmore's Luncheonette on the corner of Federal & High streets and his daughters would be known as the "Fulmore Girls". Granddad had a reputation for bringing out his shotgun for unwanted suitors so the Fulmore girls would soon marry or run off to marry their beau to get out from "Sarge".

I was raised at that mom-and-pop restaurant with my cousins, Della, Lil Mary, Albert, Van, and Vernon. While Mom was teaching me about responsibility and discipline, I was becoming an expert pinball player and best dancer at my high school, spending hours on the pinball machine and jukebox. I became a student of life, of people, and community right there and till this day, Fulmore's has the best grit ever!

At 14, Mom met the love of her life, Maurice "Big Moe", a transfer student from Washington, DC. He showed up one summer as the new boy in town. Dad rode his bike with his baseball cap on backwards and was always nicely dressed. He would hang out on the adjoining porch with his cousin Roscoe that told him about the pretty Fulmore girls next door. Roscoe told her "Bip" was visiting however, when the school year opened, Dad was in all her classes. Dad always worked and kept money in his pocket and was the first in his group to buy his first car. It was not uncommon for them to pile up the car with friends and sneak away to dance on American Band Stand. Mom said she was the feisty one so she caught my Dad's eye, and the rest would be history.

A devoted military wife, I received my fighting spirit and fearlessness through my Mother. In 1958 she once travelled for 30 days by Cargo ship from New York to France, with three babies in tow. I began to see the strength in her through me. Imagine, a young black woman in her twenties, traveling alone with babies to reunite with her husband? This was no small feat by any stretch of the imagination with the risks and dangers on the high seas. Mom showed me photos of my older siblings, wearing life preservers, at the port with her Mother-in-law, Lilian Walker and her twin sister, Aunty No-No (Nora Henry) saying their goodbyes. This was a cargo ship for sure not a luxury liner. This was the heightened period of the civil rights movement so they may have had Whites Only sections and Colored Only fountains and bathrooms. It taught me the power of womanhood and that marriage vow – 'bone of my bone and flesh of my flesh" that Mary E took to another level. Come hell or high water, Mom was determined to reunite her family!

In addition to being the enforcer, Mom was hip and all-knowing. Known as Lizzy, Aunt Mary, and Nana, she later named herself Mary E after upcoming star Mary J. Blige, with our blonde hair and iconic dance moves we would dance too. Mary E was a nurturing person with a no-nonsense temperament. It was her straight talk coupled with some good, elongated cuss words and old school phrases that kept her grandkids laughing and family members in line. Mom was funny without trying to be! There was not much that Mother could not do. She would elect to run the dialysis machine for her mother out of our home. She was very determined and could think her way out of any situation. We shared these traits as well.

As kids, we spent most of our energy trying to navigate around Mom. This was extremely hard since she had super-sonic hearing, eyes around the corner, and was an expert prosecutor. We would do things like slip out of the house, miss curfew, or invite friends over without asking permission because we knew what the answer would be from Mom. Dad was the good guy comparatively speaking, and Mom was the enforcer. As a result, her no's were no, except for my baby brother Maurice, born ten years after me on Christmas day no less, received lots of grace!

Mom always got a kick out of my life and my kids. She would tease me about my kids being born around the same time as Vanessa Williams, my Syracuse classmate however she had stopped at number three. I would later call to tell her that Vanessa had remarried and had her forth, so we were even! My mother and I were so much alike, yet I had a lot of my Dad's traits in me as well. She never let herself go as a woman, she kept herself in shape and remained fashionable. She would often tell my sister and I that if today's woman did housework like she did on her hands and knees, there would be no need for gyms. Speaking of chores, I became a feminist as a result, of having to do Saturday chores. You see, my Mother would let my brothers sleep in, however my sister and I had early morning chores. I hated it! When the guys did rise, their chores were outside doing yard work and cleaning the pool. I wanted to be outside, so I made a vow that when I grew up, I would make lots of money and not have to cook or clean. I guess you could say Mother influenced me in that way as well.

My mother and I shared her fashion sense and hairstyles. It was nothing that she worked at, she just had her own creative style and flair. Mom designed her 50th anniversary wedding gown and matching pill box hat. For my 30th wedding anniversary, I too had mine designed after an Oscar de la Renta's wedding gown. Her collection of Louis Vuitton handbags never used are vintage, you cannot buy them today because, they came from Paris, France and not made in China. Mom was the ultimate fashionista. For her home going, each female wore one of her hats in her honor as a keepsake. I was able to squeeze into one of her dresses to say my goodbyes.

Looking back, Mom was the first in the family to have a tattoo that said "Big Moe" on her leg, and the first to detect ailments with my children. I recalled, when my seven-year-old son Abdul was anxious about his upcoming eye surgery, she pulled out a coin after church and asked him to read it. "What does it say? It says, in God we trust. Exactly, put your trust in God and don't worry about tomorrow. Now keep this coin and whenever in doubt read it over again." My son smiled and breathed a sigh of relief. That was Nana, a woman of power, she never strayed far from the source. She taught me how to pray over my family, without ceasing. Mom was a prayer warrior, and the evil one was no match for her. My baby son Malcolm-Ali new her power as well, and would threaten to put her on me if I tried to discipline him as a child. Imagine that!

Mom was the reason I became the youngest charter member of Pi Mu Omega chapter of Alpha Kappa Alpha Sorority. She called me one day and told me that some ladies at church needed two more AKA's to start a local Willingboro chapter. She didn't know much about it, but she knew I was coming home to start my new job and Mom loved being an AKA's mother. That was Mom, always looking out for me and cheering me on.

I'll never forget the time I called her upset about the Trump Administration and how they were ruining government and putting billionaires in charge of government agencies. I graduated from the #1 college in the world for governmental studies, The Maxwell School of Citizenship and Public Affairs, so this was unacceptable and forbidden. Government decisions are based on community impact whereas business mindset is self-interest. I said, "Mom, the new game is billionaire status not millionaire at all. She said, ok well get off the phone and get to it! You can do it." I hung up the phone and said to my husband, I don't think Mom knows how many zeros in billion. He replied, "With your Mother it doesn't matter, she believes in you wholeheartedly.

Mom was a super planner and believed in preparation. After her death, she sent me two gifts to carry out her legacy. The first, she wrote her own Homegoing service 25 years before her death. She told her kids where it would be, but whenever we wanted to have that discussion it was too eerie. When Mom did pass, we could not find it! I recalled being upset and telling my kids about it and my daughter Divinia said, "I saw something while playing the organ one day in the bench seat." She pulled out her camera and sure enough it was a photo of my Mother's Homegoing booklet. I rushed back to the house and there it was typed since 1995, copies with all our names on it. Mother's request: all grands wear beige or pink (granddaughters same color as Mom); daughters and sons wear navy blue with beige shirt/blouse; Mom, beige lace dresses, shoes etc., second choice pink, glasses and a bible. See that Dad, looks good! It detailed songs, singers, scriptures and her own obituary. Mary E. was SOMETHING ELSE!

The second was my wedding dress, which had gone missing. It was a Demetrios by Ilissa designer wedding gown that my sorority sisters Delores Leigh and Gloria Dickerson had picked out for me. At first, I disliked that dress that took four people to carry into my dressing room. No way was I wearing that! They explained how I should wear something completely different, since I had been with Abdul forever. On my last fitting the manager said an additional $10,000 was owed as the ticket price had been mislabeled. I told them if I did not receive that gown, they would have to pay for my wedding which was in two weeks. Let's just say they gave me the gown and I ran out the store. Well, the gown goes missing and in 2021 while cleaning out my parent's attic, my brother Dennis says there's something waiting downstairs for you. It was my wedding gown, which was the missing link. Mom had always wanted her granddaughters to wear it, and Mom was in Heaven watching out for her legacies.

We shared so many attributes, keeping the family together, honoring your vows, and praying over everything and everyone. We shared so many great moments together as well. As she would age, I would come over and bring the joy. She got a kick out of hearing and laughing about my family's shenanigans, and I would put on music by her grands Divinia or Malcolm-Ali singing, and we would dance around the house. In retrospect, Mom was prepared to meet the Lord and see Big Moe, as the week of her passing, her granddaughter Destiny would style her Nana's hair and do her nails. Mom would spend her last days at my house. When my siblings commissioned me to write and design her homegoing as usual, I made it an event! Mom received a magazine cover and program ran by her grands and singing grands as well. The repast menu at Carlucci's Waterfront had her face on it and my uncle Dr. Zachary Yamba commented, "Chelley, this day has your hands all over it." Yes, except for the prettiest casket you would ever see all pink and pearly, Mom had selected nine months earlier. Of course! That was Mary E., she went out like the BOSS Chick she was! Too know me is to know my Mother.

MAURICE RUDOLPH WALKER, JR
A MAN OF VALOR, FAITH, FAMILY, FRIENDSHIP

My Daddy spoiled me. I was a Daddy's girl for sure. He influenced me in so many ways which I can sum up as he taught me about humanity, humility, and leaving a legacy. I guess you could say I was a good blend of both my parents. My Father and I were alike in many ways, he influenced my love for travel, love for meeting new people of all cultures, how to value family, loyalty, and what to look for and appreciate in a man. My deep-rooted love for my Father who was a calm man of few words, except when you crossed the line. Later, he would heavily influence who I married.

Dad was a master networker before it was "a thing". He had a black book of every person he had ever met, and he would travel on any given day or moment to see a friend or family member, unannounced. Basically, it didn't matter if they were at home because he had back up numbers for days. Of course, Mary E. had her fair share of traveling and was not interested in road trips whatsoever. So, Dad would take the kids on a trip to who knows where. He too knew the best way to navigate around her No's was to just do it! Rather than spend days or weeks trying to change her mind, it was easier to just suffer the consequences. He even had a second home built in Denver, CO without telling her. When he presented it to her six months later, he said "we can keep the home in New Jersey just give me three years to see if you like it. That's where I got it from. The first time I brought my now husband home with me from college, I did not ask my Mother either, but rather had my boyfriend show up with me, with his suitcase, unannounced. My Mother was pissed, however, Dad on the other hand was cool with it and told him not to worry, then gave him the keys to his car for the weekend. That was my Dad!

Dad was from Washington, D.C. so he had that D.C. swag. Always dressed to the nines and about his business, not that shucking and jiving type you often run across, he was a manly man, huge in stature yet mild mannered, a gentleman. I learned to be a social butterfly by watching my Dad bring people around and introduce me to my new auntie or uncle of some sort! He had buddies from all over and Dad would also fly to other countries and could navigate quite well without a map. My brother Dennis told me the story of when he was stationed in Germany, and how 'Dad showed up one weekend unannounced and asked to borrow his car for the weekend. Dad drove over to France to locate the former babysitter to direct him to my Brother Larry's gravesite. My Dad was legendary for his travel excursions, which I shared my Dad's love for travel.

I had the greatest upbringing in our military community. My Dad spoiled us by putting in a built-in pool, so that we could entertain at home during the hot summer months. He loved gadgets and cars, so we had the best Christmas presents and automobiles. One Christmas we each got an instrument to play like the Jackson Five. I hated my present as it was a trumpet. I cried that morning as my sister received a flute. You see, I just knew my big lips would grow bigger, little did I know that my lips would later become "trendy" and culturally appropriated, and be worth billions of dollars in cosmetic surgery. I'm still waiting for big noses to become fashionable. I was horrible at playing the trumpet and each year I tried out for the RV High School band, and did not make the cut. My final year I begged the band director to make my Dad happy and it happened. My Dad was at every game cheering me on with his camera. Little did he know I wasn't really playing as I had worked it out with the director in my favor. I still have that trumpet on my fireplace mantle. One day I plan to take up lessons and do my Dad the honors by playing "Taps".

My first car was a Cadillac, passed down to me by my Dad's father who lived in Washington, DC. I received my middle name Clarice after his wife, Aunt Clara and the family name Maurice. I would spend every summer in DC and therefore when my grandfather passed, I was the one quite naturally, to receive his car. It was hardly ever driven as they had a driver for occasional Sunday outings. That car lasted one year with me. Like in the movie Cooley High it was always packed with my girls and we would cruise to school and parties. I was just like my Dad for sure.

My Dad love gadgets and we always had the newest stereo

equipment, cameras and video equipment. My Dad always filmed everything we did as a family. Thinking about it now, that's why I have over 10,000 photos and videos on my phone, my dad influenced me to document everything as a personal history and life experience. He made home movies and would invite friends and family over. Usually, the film would break, or the projector would overheat, or a bulb would blow but it didn't matter.

One of my fondest memories with my Father was my wedding day. I had a horse drawn carriage that picked me up at the house and rode my Dad and me to Wesley A.M.E. Zion Church. It took us over 2 hours and my dad held the umbrella over my head to shield the sun. I felt like Miss America as we waved to passersby. Yep, he spoiled me but not spoiled rotten. I was his Princess.

My Dad taught me humility. Every holiday he would pick up a stray family and bring them home to have holiday meals with us. They would later become our adopted family. God called him home on October 22, 2019, Retired Staff Sergeant Maurice R. Walker Jr., a devout family man affectionately known by friends and loved ones as "Big Moe" and "Junie". Maurice was born to the late Maurice Walker Sr. and the late Lillian Walker in Mt. Holly, New Jersey in 1935. From this union they had two children, Maurice and his younger sister Patricia known as "Trish". Maurice spent his earlier years in Newport News Virginia, Binghamton, and Washington, DC. However he was raised on Earl Street in Burlington City, New Jersey where he met his lovely wife Mary Fulmore. Their romance would develop as a fairytale.

Maurice attended Wilbur Watts High School in Burlington City and was a natural born athlete in track and field. As a young man he had a paper route and would deliver "The Burlington Press". Maurice retired from the military after 20 years in 1974, then retired again from National Gypsum. From there he was determined to join the ranks of Black business owners that were prevalent during the 70's and 80's.

My Dad would later influence me to become an entrepreneur. Dad felt that financial independence was the better route to take and would soon open his own business just like his father-in-law (Fulmore's Luncheonette), his uncle (E.J. Flippen Funeral Home), cousin "Sonny" Burroughs (corner store in Philadelphia) and another cousin "Sonny" Nesmith (Dry Cleaners) that would serve as his mentor. Dad opened his own family business in Burlington and named it "M & M Dry Cleaners" (after him and his soul mate Mary). I also get my humanitarian spirit from my dad. He would dry clean the clothing and provide free delivery service, oftentimes "benevolently" to his customers. He was constantly trying to help his community by being charitable, and his heart for the people would parlay into real estate, as he would purchase homes for extended family members to rent, in need of a decent place to stay.

My Dad wanted me to go into the military which I refused however he did influence me to go into public service. He was an active member of American Legion Post 509 in Westhampton and Post 336 in Burlington. For over 30 years, he would recruit young men to send away to American Legion Jersey "Boys State", as a strong tradition of patriotism, and excellence in the development of tomorrows leaders. Starting with my brother Maurice, it would become a family tradition and every grandson would attend including Darnell, Dwayne, Jason, Dennis Jr., Martin-Abdul, and Malcolm-Ali.

THE DAVIS 6

I was not looking for a husband, but God sent him to me. My day 1, Martin "Abdul" Davis my ride or die, husband, affectionately called "Hubster", for 35 years and counting, taught me about "two becoming one" and pushing past all the obstacles. We are the Mary E. and the Maurice duo of the family. Our four amazing kids, Divinia, Martin-Abdul, Destiny, and Malcolm-Ali taught me about sacrifice and unconditional love.

Through them I learned to become less selfish and more self-less. When Malcolm-Ali received his degree at Syracuse University on May 13, 2018 it marked the end of an era. He became the fourth of the Davis siblings to graduate from SU. His parents are proud Syracuse alumni and philanthropist that have helped raised hundreds of thousands of dollars for black and brown student scholarships. They encouraged their children to continue the legacy. Michelle's cousin Horace Morris was the first African-American to attend SU on a football scholarship in 1948. While the Davis 6 enjoy a truly unique Orange bond, they value the way that bond extends beyond their immediate family to other alums. The Davis 6 enabled me to leave a rich heritage at Syracuse University and have a direct impact on 8 chancellors that served at the University. We made sure that black students were represented on campus and had the same opportunities and access as the other students. We had each other's back for over 40 years and counting.

***

This manuscript is dedicated to my parents, the Davis 6, my husband Martin Abdul Davis our beloved children Divinia, Abdul, Destiny, Malcolm-Ali, bonus sons, William Young and Abdul's LBs, all future grandchildren, and legacies. My siblings, Dennis, Maureen, Lamont, Maurice, my sister-in-loves Tara, JanNa, Bonnie, Diane, Terry, Tammy, Beverly, my nieces and nephews, Darnell, Agulanda, Dwayne, Sheena, Jason, Danielle, Dennis Jr. and Ronita, Kiana, Maurice II, Demetrius, Hannah; three angelic grandnieces and nephew, Edyn, Kyla, Ava and Ari, uncle Dr. Zachary Yamba; aunts Shirley Steed, and Kay Moses-Turner. All my cousins, the Flippen Family, The Fulmore's, The Walkers, Shivers and Davis family. My line sisters, sorority sisters, Syracuse CBT family, DeLoise Lewis, my wedding party, Dr. Honey, Reverend James, RV classmates, Wesley AME Zion Church, New Jerusalem House of God, The Perfecting Church, and those that believed in me and those that did not. Mentors Reverend James, Dr. Honey, Larry Martin, Stan "The Man" Matthews, and Dr. Frazier. The name above all names, my Lord and Savior, Jesus Christ. "God is with me – Be strong and courageous, and do the work. Do not be afraid or discouraged, for the Lord God, my God, is with you." ~ 1 Chronicles 28:20

Professor Michelle Walker-Davis, MPA/MS is a serial entrepreneur and a servant leader. She is the Managing Partner for IMG, a grant development firm in the $850B marketplace. Prior companies include rehabbing homes and managing entertainers. A real estate developer and franchise owner, she is on a mission to recirculate the $3T dollars within the Black community and raise the value of women. A survivor of several life-threatening automobile accidents, she now uses her second chances and total existence to fulfill God's plan for her life to use her global influence to transform lives and change the world. The founder and visionary behind Women of Power and Transformation (WOPAT) "1 Billion Successful Women Entrepreneurs Worldwide" initiative. A proud member of Alpha Kappa Alpha Sorority, Inc., founder of Rich Woman Society, AACCNJ, hosts a podcast "Fresh Money Talk", national leader with MBN, and investor with Black Broadway. A former Assistant Professor, and Senior Congressional Evaluator with GAO, she wrote 10 Congressional reports. Whether it's impacting women and girls around the world, delivering keynotes, winning grants or raising funds for education, her mission is bigger than self, it's to make a universal impact. To this end, she created an annual Game-Changers Award recognizing Women of Power and Men of Valor. She eagerly serves as an Alumni Ambassador and helped raise millions for Endowed Scholarships at Syracuse University. She is married to her college sweetheart and business partner of 35 years, and they are the proud parents of four amazing young professionals. All are alumni of SU and known as the "Davis 6".

www.ingramcontent.com/pod-product-compliance
Lightning Source LLC
Chambersburg PA
CBHW061736270326
41928CB00011B/2263